Elmer Towns

The 8 Laws of Leadership

Making Extraordinary Leaders out of Ordinary Believers

Church Growth Institute
Providing Practical Tools for Growth
P.O. Box 4404, Lynchburg, VA 24502

D1052693

Editor: Cindy G. Spear
Designers: Carolyn R. Phelps
          Jim Copeland
Editorial and Design
Assistant: Tamara Johnson

Unless otherwise noted, all Scriptures
in this text are the King James Version.

**Dedicated
to
John Maxwell
Pastor of Skyline Wesleyan Church
Greater San Diego, California**

I do not know of a greater pastoral leader than John Maxwell. He demonstrates leadership by attitude and actions, and knows why and how he is leading his people. This means he has a great knowledge of the task of leadership.

I have received his Injoy tapes on leadership from the beginning of the series. They are excellent. I recommend them to pastors all the time. As a matter of fact, John has helped clarify my task of leadership as well as my understanding of how it works. Some of my own skills in leadership were learned through trial and error. As I listen to John Maxwell, he puts into words how I believed and acted. I have quoted him in this material more than anyone because he is the authority on the subject. At times I am not sure where my thoughts end and his begin. I don't want credit for anything that belongs to John Maxwell, so let's give him *all* the credit – because he is the living authority on the topic.

Therefore: John, because you let Christ lead you, because your leadership of the pastoral staff at Skyline makes them one of the best in America, because of your outstanding leadership of the people at Skyline to grow in grace and grow in numbers, and because of your knowledge in leadership skills, I dedicate this book to you – John Maxwell the leader.

Elmer Towns

Elmer L. Towns

CONTENTS

PREFACE

PREFACE

The issue of leadership is a growing concern in the church. Many pastors and church leaders today study the principles of leadership and the examples of great leaders with a view of becoming better leaders.

Ghandi, the Prime Minister of India, was a creative leader, yet his power was the simple attraction of vast multitudes of people who followed him. Ghandi led the world's second largest nation, India, out from the control of what was then the world's most powerful empire, the British empire. Mao exhibited extraordinary leadership when he led the world's largest number of people, mainland China, into Communism. During the early days of the Second World War, Winston Churchill led his tiny island nation against the unchecked vicious aggression of Adolf Hitler's army as it swallowed up Europe. In the 1960s Martin Luther King, Jr., challenged America's prejudice, tradition, and antiquated laws that kept black America in social bondage. He personified the ultimate law of leadership – the law of dreams – with his cry, "I have a dream" – the watchword of his leadership.

The church has also produced great leaders in this century. Perhaps the single most influencial church leader in the first half of this century was Henrietta Mears. While she is unknown by most, Henrietta Mears, the Director of Christian Education at Hollywood Presbyterian Church in Hollywood, California, taught a Sunday School class of up to 500 college-age students. Many of them did great things for God and became great leaders in their own rank. Also, Henrietta Mears helped establish Forest Home, a Christian conference center. She influenced some of the greatest Christian leaders and movements of our day, including Bill Bright who founded Campus Crusade for Christ; the late Dawson Trotman who began the Navigators; and even Billy Graham who was influenced for God at Forest Home just prior to the Los Angeles Crusade which gave birth to his high-profile, international ministry as an evangelist.

Dr. Lee Robertson said, "Everything rises or falls on leadership." He recognized that growing churches are led by growing leaders. But this statement may also be applied to our families and businesses. "*Everything* rises or falls on leadership." Therefore, becoming a better leader will have far-reaching effects in every aspect of your life.

Just what is a leader? Let's clear up some misconceptions. A leader is not an office or position, a rule-maker, a speech-maker, a manager, an administrator or organizer, nor a spiritual gift. A leader may have some or all of these characteristics, but what characteristic does every leader have? A true leader is able to *influence* and relate to other people. He or she is able to persuade others to follow.

Today, the leadership role and duties of the pastor are changing. In the rural days, he annually visited every member, dropped by the hospital, buried the dead, counseled the bereaved, prayed with new babies, and married the young. He did it because that is the way ministers have always done it.

But Boomers are pastoring to a different exegetical drum beat. They see in the New Testament a different job for pastors than World War II-oriented pastors before them. The older pastor was a leader of people, but the newer pastor is a leader of leaders.

John Maxwell describes the pastor as a Red Cross worker going to war, rather than a general of an artillery division heading for an attack. The older pastor thinks of himself as a general, but every time he passes a wounded soldier, he stops his jeep, causing the division of ranks behind him to grind to a halt while he bandages up the wounded. Then back into the jeep the general climbs and the division starts up again for battle, only to be halted when the general sees another wounded soldier in the field.

While the ranks wait for the general, the battle could be turning against him or even exposing the ranks to destruction because they are not in battle formation. A general is a leader of leaders. He leads a medical officer who in turn leads the medical corpsman, the one who should care for the wounded. The pastor should be a general, not just a medical corpsman.

The new role of pastoral leadership emphasizes management of lay workers, church resources, the church calendar, and money. This new role for church pastors centers on *leadership*.

This book is about leadership, not what Baby Boomers want, not what older pastors do, and not the type of leadership that is operative in today's world.

This book is about *true* leadership; the type of leader found in the New Testament, the mature leader who touches all bases while building his followers, building his organization and reaching his objectives.

This book is not about pastor-dictators. I started listing the 100 largest Sunday Schools in 1968 and have seen pastor-dictators come and go. Outwardly they get the job done. The bottom-line numbers make them look like great leaders. But their works collapse around them as they lose their numbers and many lose their ministries. People follow a dictator only for a limited time.

I remember one such leader who reached 1,100 in attendance during the height of the busing explosion. His people loved him because they loved his success. But the busing explosion resulted in an explosion in his church. When the church voted, there were 300 members voting, not the 800 children who rode the buses. The members questioned the pastor's attendance numbers, his methods, and finally him. When the people voted, the pastor lost. Then he shouted:

"Get out of my church..."

He made his demand stick because the church was registered in his name. The pastor-dictator owns the work, owns the facilities, and thinks he owns the people.

The emerging pastor-leader is no dictator. He has learned to share his leadership with his people, through shared decision-making, shared problem-solving, and shared goal-setting.

Shared Leadership
1. Shared decision-making.
2. Shared problem-solving.
3. Shared goal-setting.

Not all of the older pastors were dictators. As a matter of fact, very few were dictators. Since a dictator has "maximum power," the former pastors who got their example from the rural settings actually had little power, if any. They certainly did not have "maximum power."

Pastoral Leadership Models

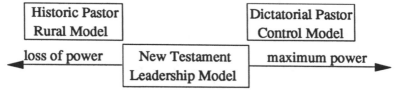

The pastor-leader is one who "leads his sheep beside still waters," as the Lord would lead people. The pastor/leader is one who "putteth his sheep out, and leadeth them out."

Don't confuse the pastor-dictator and the pastor-leader. They are both strong, effective, productive, and persuasive. Just because a jet plane looks like a glider, does not mean it is the same thing. To get off the ground a jet is pushed and a glider is pulled.

Dictators and leaders both get the job done. However, dictators do it the wrong way; leaders do it the right way.

I have friends who are or were pastor-dictators. I appreciate what they have accomplished, if in fact their accomplishments were for Christ. I will not use information gained personally through those friends to anyone's disadvantage. Since no one is perfect, I pray daily, "Forgive us our debts, as we forgive our debtors."

I have friends who are pastor/leaders. I appreciate what they have done for Christ. I will use some of them as illustrations because I believe it is to their advantage and to the advantage of the church.

I wrote this book to help all who are or will be pastors or lay leaders to become better leaders. I am not naive. I know that just reading a book about leadership will not make anyone a better leader, because good leadership involves knowing people, cultures, history, and local turf. So this book won't *make* the reader a leader. But as John Maxwell says, "Leaders are readers," so this book can become a standard by which you measure your leadership skills and understanding. Learning about leadership is a first step toward growing as a leader.

If I had written this book as a very young preacher, I may have shown leadership leaning toward total board control in the church. I was a young Presbyterian pastor who understood little about leadership influence and little about the proper expression of Presbyterian government.

If I had written this book as a middle-age Baptist who was intoxicated with the first days of the mega-church movement, I may have leaned toward the pastor-dictator because I saw their accomplishment.

Now I trust I've come to a balanced view of leadership. It is located between "abuse of power" and "abdicating power." Since power is always located in God and communicated through His Word, leadership is about properly using power.

I want to credit John Maxwell for giving me more cognitive information about leadership than any other one person. Not only does Maxwell understand leadership, he role-models it to the staff and people of Skyline Wesleyan Church in Greater San Diego, California. I want to thank the pastors in the *Ten Innovative*

Churches for allowing me to interview them about their leadership styles. They sharpened my view of leadership. I want to thank every pastor who is my friend for their desire to lead people. No matter what their view of leadership, they've had to put up with a lot of junk just to be a pastor. I also want to thank Doug Porter, who was my graduate assistant, for typing and edifying the original manuscript.

The core of this book came out of a series of lectures I gave in the summer of 1990 to the Eastern Michigan Nazarene Conference at Indian Lake Nazarene Camp near Lansing, Michigan.

I give credit for all that is good in this book to the influence of others and take the blame for all its weakness.

May this book accomplish its goal – to contribute to better leadership in our churches.

Elmer Towns
Lynchburg, Virginia
Summer 1992

Overview

THE EIGHT LAWS
OF LEADERSHIP

OVERVIEW: THE EIGHT LAWS OF LEADERSHIP

Law One: The Law of Dreams	
Descriptive Statement	People follow a leader who directs them to a desirable objective.
Prescriptive Statement	The leader must direct followers to a desirable objective.
Slogan	When people buy into your dreams, they buy into your leadership.

Law Two: The Law of Rewards	
Descriptive Statement	People follow a leader who provides them rewards from their self-chosen goals.
Prescriptive Statement	The leader must reward those who follow him.
Slogan	The things that get rewarded, get done.

Law Three: The Law of Credibility	
Descriptive Statement	People follow a leader when they have confidence in his plans.
Prescriptive Statement	The leader must have a credibility plan to reach the objective.
Slogan	The leader who believes in his followers has people who believe in him.

Law Four: The Law of Communication	
Descriptive Statement	People follow a leader who effectively communicates his plan to reach the objective.
Prescriptive Statement	The leader must effectively communicate his plans to reach the objective.
Slogan	People follow a leader who gives clear directions to his followers.

Law Five: The Law of Accountability	
Descriptive Statement	People follow a leader who gives them responsibility to help reach the objective.
Prescriptive Statement	The leader must know the contribution that his followers make to help reach the goal.
Slogan	People don't do what you expect, but what you inspect.

Law Six: The Law of Motivation	
Descriptive Statement	People follow a leader who gives them compelling reasons to reach the objective.
Prescriptive Statement	The leader must motivate followers to accomplish the objective.
Slogan	People follow you when you give them a reason to work.

Law Seven: The Law of Problem-Solving	
Descriptive Statement	People follow a leader who gives solutions to problems that hinder them from reaching the objective.
Prescriptive Statement	The leader must solve problems that hinder followers from reaching their objective.
Slogan	The more barriers that frustrate your followers, the less likely they are to reach the goal.

Law Eight: The Law of Decision-Making	
Descriptive Statement	People follow a leader who gives answers to the decisions involving their objective.
Prescriptive Statement	The leader must make good decisions that move followers toward the objective.
Slogan	Leaders make good decisions on good information, bad decisions on bad information, and lucky decisions on no information.

Chapter One

THE LAW OF DREAMS

Chapter One

THE LAW OF DREAMS

Great leaders lead by planting dreams in the hearts of followers. When Jesus "saw the multitudes, He was moved with compassion for them" (Matt. 9:36). Jesus' vision of people moved Him to action. His vision of people motivated Him to preach His greatest sermon, the Sermon on the Mount (Matt. 5:1ff). His vision of people motivated Him to give His greatest call for prayer, a prayer for workers (Matt. 9:38). Finally, His vision motivated Him to give His greatest challenge, a call to make disciples of all nations (Matt. 28:18-20).

Both vision and dreams (the law uses dreams and vision interchangeably) describe the first mandate of leaders. "A leader must direct people to a desirable objective." To state it in everyday language, "When people buy into your dreams, they buy into your leadership."

Law One: The Law of Dreams	
Descriptive Statement	People follow a leader who directs them to a desirable objective.
Prescriptive Statement	The leader must direct followers to a desirable objective.
Slogan	When people buy into your dreams, they buy into your leadership.

The dream of Martin Luther King, Jr., ignited the black community of the United States. "I have a dream," he cried from the front of the Washington Monument in the nation's capital to over one million listening ears. The civil rights leader was an Old Testament seer (prophet). He saw "a little black boy and a little white boy in Georgia play together." The dream of King led to the passing of Civil Rights legislation giving equality to a disenfranchized minority. He epitomized leadership by leading a nation to legally abolish the pervasive barrier of inequality that was practiced in America.

When the black community bought into King's dream, they made him their uncontested leader. They endured the police dogs that were released on them. They did not give up when fire hoses were turned on them. Many went to jail for the dream. It was a dream of freedom. When the legislators bought into King's dreams, they enacted the laws needed to carry out those dreams. The most powerful tool a leader possesses is dreams.

In the Old Testament, prophets led the nations without the sword, legislative office or political might. They led with a thunderous voice. They spoke for God. Prophets were called seers (1 Sam. 9:9) or dreamers (Gen. 37:19). They were jeered, mocked, and stoned. Some were sawed in half, starved or beheaded.

THE PROPHETIC SEER
He saw first.
He saw furthest into the future.
He saw most.

The law of dreams gives direction to leaders. Their dreams give them motivation, direction, and purpose. But lack of a dream or vision destroys the leadership of anyone. "Where there is no vision, the people perish" (Prov. 29:18). People will follow you when you have a dream or vision, especially if your dream is their dream. But they flounder without a dream.

WHAT DREAMS GIVE LEADERS
Motivation to lead.
Direction to go.
Purpose to pay the price.

In the business community, the first law of leadership is described as "management by objectives (MBO)." Business people give leadership to their company by focusing on objectives. The objective is the supreme consideration in making management decisions.

THE STRENGTH OF OBJECTIVES

They make followers future oriented.
They make followers forward (action) oriented.
They make followers (bottom-line) result-oriented.

Bill Munroe was leading the singing in his church in Indianapolis when he felt God calling him to return to his home state of South Carolina to start a new church. He packed his belongings in a rental truck and began his trip south with his family. About half-way there, he and his wife stopped at a roadside picnic area to have lunch. Over lunch, he began to describe his dream of a church.

"I'm going to build a church on 20 acres of ground," he began. "I can see Pine trees, Live Oak trees, with hanging Spanish moss. The church will be a big square yellow brick building that will seat 1,000 to 1,200 people. In one corner, there will be a high pulpit from which I will preach. I can see the building full of people, sitting on red padded pews, listening to me preach the Gospel."

That was 1969. The dream began when Bill Munroe put a plastic name tag on his lapel which read, "Bill Munroe, Pastor, Florence Baptist Temple." He walked into the K-Mart parking lot inviting people to a vacant theatre that he and his wife had cleaned for the first service on a deserted military base.

Today, as you drive south of Florence, South Carolina, on the east side of U.S. 301, there is a yellow brick church building that will seat about 1,200, situated on 30 acres of land. There are Pine trees and Live Oak trees with Spanish moss. When you enter the auditorium, the pulpit is up high in one corner of the building, facing rows of red padded pews. On a typical Sunday, there are about 1,200 people listening to Bill Munroe preach the Gospel.

Great works for God began as dreams in the minds of the leaders. Leaders can only lead their followers to achieve what they can first conceive. The opposite is also true: You won't achieve what you can't conceive!

What to Dream

When you dream, you first need an overall dream or vision of what you want to do with your life. When a young couple stands before a minister to be married, they come with their dreams. They dream of owning a house, raising a family, and living together in harmony. When a young person begins a business, he too has a dream. His dream grows out of and impacts his way of doing things. He may envision the size of the staff, the type of building, and the landscape of the property. Usually, when people begin a new business, they have a dream of the money they will make. While that selfish goal may not motivate the employees or customers, what they get will surely motivate them. The owner usually measures his dream by increased productivity, enlarged distribution or new markets and products.

How to Make Goals

Dreams are usually vague, and at times mysterious. You know what you want, but you cannot always describe it exactly as Pastor Bill Munroe did for his wife. Most leaders are not as eloquent as Martin Luther King, Jr., when he described little black and little white boys playing together in Georgia.

There are four steps to becoming an effective leader. First, you must dream dreams which give focus to your leadership. Second, out of your dreams come specific goals. These specific goals give quantitative direction for your leadership. Third, plans are the route you take to get people to the goal. Finally, tactics or production are the actual steps to move people along.

DREAMS →GOALS →PLANS → TACTICS

To be a good manager, you only focus on plans and tactics, but good leaders focus on dreams and goals. Successful leaders take the long-range view. Leaders are dreamers who light fires in the hearts of followers. Bureaucrats manage people, but accomplish little. True leaders inspire people to sacrifice their leisure, their sleep, their money, sometimes even their health or life. Why? Because they buy into a dream, the dream of both leader and follower.

Goals Give Direction

Goals may be defined as dreams with deadlines. They are dreams with dates, dreams with statistics or dreams with limitations. If you can't put numbers, places, and faces to your dreams, you're just a dreamer. The world is filled with little boys who dream of being a doctor and of little girls who dream of becoming Miss America. And you too will be just a dreamer if you cannot get direction from your dream. Learning to express your dreams with goals will motivate you to accomplish some of your dreams.

Leaders must be goal-setters. First, leaders must set *long-range goals*. These give an enduring view of the organization or movement. They keep hope alive and give direction to plans. Long-range goals tell us where we want to be in five or ten years. Because of their longevity, they give stability to the group following the leader.

A new church sets a goal of purchasing 20 acres, constructing an auditorium, educational facilities, gymnasium, and retirement complex. Because it will take over twelve years to complete the project, they are called long-range goals. Young couples sit on folding chairs in rented facilities and sacrifice their money to the infant church because they believe in the dream as expressed in long-range goals.

Short-range goals are what you want to accomplish this Christmas through a music program or the evangelistic goals of the summer through Vacation Bible School, camp, and backyard Bible clubs. Short-range goals mobilize us for immediate action and call for instant response.

Leaders should use two other types of goals also. *Input goals* are those things a leader and follower will do to get a program or meeting going. To plan a city-wide meeting, the leader has an input goal of putting a flyer in every front door, getting an announcement in the newspaper six times, and getting the teens to post 200 posters announcing the meeting. Input goals give meaning, direction to activity, and they should be based on predictable results.

Output goals are the bottom-line results we expect from the meeting. We expect 50 people to make a decision at the city-wide crusade, 20 for salvation and 30 for rededication. We will follow up the people making decisions and "bond" 12 new people or four new families to the church.

When you make your goals, make SMART goals. The word *smart* is an acrostic to help you prepare goals. Goals should be Specific, Measurable, Attainable, Realistic, and Time-Related.

SMART GOALS	
S	pecific
M	easurable
A	ttainable
R	ealistic
T	ime-Related

People are motivated to follow a leader who uses specific goals such as planning to reach a specific number of people (i.e., 18). He has direction and purpose to his leadership. He makes goals measurable so that followers will be motivated by quantitative steps. If attendance is currently averaging 82, there will be a total of 100 people when he reaches the goal of 18 people. Goals should be attainable in the circumstances. Do not plan to have 100 in a Sunday School class that will seat only 20 and averages an attendance of 10. Also, plan realistic goals about which everyone feels good. People will only work to achieve a goal they have adopted as their own. Goals need to be related to a time and date. Plan to reach 18 people in the next six months or year rather than just planning to reach 18 people sometime in the unknown future.

To become financially independent is not a dream that will become a reality by just dreaming. You must set a goal of learning a trade or profession, graduating from college, getting the right job at the right place. You must work harder than those around you and make sacrifices to reach your goal. You must learn to save money and to invest money. You must discipline your life, control your money, in order to control your destiny.

A young minister might set a goal to build a church of 1,000 members. He must translate his dream to an interim goal of winning 100 people for Christ this year.

Everyone must have a dream, but you are just a dreamer unless your dreams become measurable, attainable, specific goals. Then goals must be translated into actual plans.

Plans That Work

Goals lead you to make plans. If you don't have workable plans to carry out your specific goals, you are still a dreamer.

To accomplish your goals, you need several kinds of plans. Long-range plans determine your general direction for the next several years. Develop an annual calendar to show what you intend to do this year and when you will do it. Short-range plans reveal your strategy for the next several weeks. A weekly calendar reveals your schedule for the next seven days. A "things to do" list will identify your plans for today.

"You may not do all your dreams, but you will probably do no more than your dreams."

The same can be said for goals. You may not accomplish all your goals, but you will probably not accomplish anything without goals.

The same is true of plans. You won't accomplish all your plans, but you probably won't accomplish anything without plans. A friend once told me, "You have to see a dream and say a dream (goals) before you can ever seize a dream (plans)."

How to Make Your Dreams Biblical

How can you make your dreams biblical? Make your dreams express biblical ideals. A pastor might dream of saturating his community with the Gospel (Acts 5:28), seeing his church grow in the Word (Acts 2:42), and motivating his people to win the lost to Christ (Acts 1:8). He might envision a time when his people are involved in a cell group for fellowship, Bible study or pastoral care. He might dream of young people surrendering to the call of God for ministry or his church significantly influencing the laws of his community.

Dreams are expressions of biblical faith. Paul spoke of moving "from faith to faith" (Rom 1:17), meaning we move from our initial saving faith in Christ to a living faith. To "live by faith" is to let God accomplish what He has promised. When we as leaders express biblical faith, we begin to move our followers to that same faith. Faith is affirming what God has said in His Word. Abraham had strong faith "being fully convinced that what He (God) had promised He was also able to perform" (Rom. 4:21). Abraham became a leader of his family, and ultimately of a tribe of people, because of his strong faith. Abraham lived "from faith to faith" and experienced many faith events in his life when he saw God intervene and accomplish great things.

Plan a biblical strategy to accomplish your dreams. Plans place actual steps to goals and dreams. Plans control your goals – goals control your dreams. Therefore, plan biblical strategies that will accomplish your goals and turn your dreams into reality.

Tactics Pay Off

The final step is tactics or actually working out the dream. Martin Luther King, Jr., had a dream, but he also had the backing of lawyers at the NAACP who set goals of winning court challenges. They made plans to work out their day-to-day strategy. Then King had an army of people who marched from Selma, Alabama, who registered voters, solicited finances, and did a thousand other tasks to make the dream a reality.

How to Make Your Dreams Come True

Making your dreams come true involves more than wishing upon a star. Making plans is the first step to realizing your dreams. When a pastor dreams of building a great church, he needs to use the laws of God, not fight them or violate them. The pastor is working in two worlds, so he needs to recognize the principles that operate in each sphere. There are two kinds of laws; first, spiritual laws that operate in the spiritual world and second, the laws that control this world. The two do not naturally contradict each other, but when it appears they do, it is because man has wrongly understood or applied them. Therefore, the pastor must make plans in keeping with the laws that control both worlds.

One law to understand in making plans is the Law of the Division of Labor. This law states that God will not do for His people what is their responsibility and within their realm. People must do for themselves, then trust God to accomplish what they cannot do. God reserves certain tasks as His tasks. While God can do anything He desires, He will normally not do something He has delegated to us. God could win people to Himself without our involvement, but He has called us to make disciples of all nations. When we witness and share the Gospel with lost people, we are doing what God has commanded us to do. Then God does what only He can do and forgives their sins, gives them a new nature, and ultimately takes them to heaven.

THE LAW OF THE DIVISION OF LABOR

You cannot do the work God has reserved as His own task.
God will not do the work for you
that He has given as your task.

Leaders also need to understand the Law of Blessability. God's blessing is not primarily based upon doctrine, correct exegesis or separated lives. God blesses those who yield to Him, pray, exercise faith, and serve Him with all their hearts. God blesses those who correctly relate to Him and worship Him. If we want to be used of God and experience the blessing of God in our life and ministry, we should be concerned about developing our internal relationship with Him.

> ## THE LAW OF BLESSABILITY
>
> *God does not necessarily bless doctrine, programs,*
> *methods or avoidance of sin.*
> *God blesses those who are close to His heart*
> *in love, faith, and hope.*

The third law for leaders is the Law of Causation. This law states that a work of God is always caused, it never just happens. Leaders have to take the initiative to cause the work for God to go forward. Sometimes others might think a great work of God has just happened, but that is because they do not see the prayers, sacrifices, and labors that others have put into making that work of God happen. To realize your dreams, learn to plan your work and work your plans. Then your dreams can become a reality.

> ## THE LAW OF CAUSATION
>
> *Nothing in the work of God just happens.*
> *It is caused.*

Leaders must build their work on the Law of Laws. Accordingly, the work of God is accomplished by following His natural and spiritual laws. It is wrong to pray and ask God to break His law as an exception for you. A person cannot fall from a tall ladder and pray to miss the ground or fall upward. Christians must learn to live by God's laws, not look for exceptions. If you want to see your dreams come true, pray for God to use His laws, not violate them or cancel them for you. Make plans based on the laws by which God generally governs His universe.

THE LAW OF LAWS

God does not run His work by chance, but by His laws. We prosper as we follow His laws and encounter difficulty when we violate these laws.

Dreams give energy for life. There are several reasons why we get renewed zeal from our dreams. First, your dreams motivate you to action. Second, goals which grow out of your dreams guide you in your planning. Third, plans you develop to accomplish your goals will give credibility to your dreams. As a result, people will enthusiastically work according to the strategy planned to accomplish the goals and make the dream a reality.

Many pastors have dried on the vine and lost their burden for ministry. These pastors begin as young men with great dreams, but lose their vision along the way. Every pastor needs three churches. The first church is where he learns. There he makes his mistakes and learns how to do ministry. The people understand that their young pastor is just out of college and this is his first church. They seem willing to overlook many of his mistakes and remain supportive. They may even tell him he is the best preacher they have ever heard. Their support builds his dreams and motivates him to go on in life. The second church is where the pastor can really minister. There he applies the lessons he learned in his first church and meets people's needs through ministry. In this second church, he carries out his daily dreams. The third church is one He never attains, but is the church of his dreams. For this church he strives but never arrives. There he dreams great things for God. When a pastor loses his dream, he loses his purpose in life and he loses his following.

EVERY PASTOR NEEDS THREE CHURCHES

1. A church to learn from.
2. A church to minister to.
3. A church to dream on.

How to Keep Your Dreams Alive

Young Timothy apparently struggled to keep his dreams alive. Paul wrote to him and urged, "Neglect not the gift that is in thee, which was given thee by prophecy, with the laying on of the hands of the presbytery" (1 Tim. 4:14). As Timothy heard Paul preach, he dreamed of the ministry he would himself have someday. Later, the church encouraged him, commissioned him, and followed him. But in the midst of his ministry, Timothy became discouraged. Paul wrote again, "Therefore I remind you to stir up the gift of God which is in you through the laying on of my hands" (2 Tim. 1:6). Timothy had acquired the tools he needed for ministry through his long association with the apostle. Now Paul urged him to use those tools to make his dreams a reality.

HOW TO BE A GREAT LEADER

Read great books.
Visit great places.
Attend great events.
Talk to great people.

Read great books. When you read the biographies of those who have accomplished their dreams, you are motivated to do the same. When you read the great devotional classics which have brought revival to other lives, you too stir up your ashes into flames. When you read the Bible, the great book, it becomes your source of even greater dreams.

Visit great places. Many pastors like to visit churches and stand behind the pulpits of pastors who have done what they dreamed of doing. Visit the places where George Whitefield, John Wesley, Charles Spurgeon, D. L. Moody, Jerry Falwell, W. A. Criswell, and others preached. Visit the sites of great events in Christianity; Hebron where Abraham built his altar, Jerusalem, Bethlehem, Calvary, and the Garden tomb. There is something about standing in a place where you know God has previously worked. It encourages you to dream of what you want to do for God and what God can do through you.

Attend great events. We live in the greatest days of history. Some of the greatest things ever done for God are being done today. Become involved in great events by your attendance. If you think the power of God is going to fall, be there. Don't get it over religious television programs. Don't plan to listen to the tape. Be there and feel God's anointing for yourself. If you want to be a great man or woman of God, go and experience great events.

Talk to great people. The only difference between you today and you ten years from now is the books you read and the people you meet. Just as a poker gets hot when placed in the flame, so you will become like those with whom you associate. If you want to be a great man or woman of God, get next to great men and women of God who are on fire for God. Let their fire warm you.

What Dreams Will Do for You

Your dreams will make you future oriented. We don't need churches that live off history lessons. Too often churches live in the past, remembering "the good old days" when revival swept through their towns. The greatest thing to remember about yesterday was that it ended last night. You are not going to live in yesterday. You are going to live in tomorrow. The people who are going to do something for God are future oriented. They dream of God using them to impact their communities. Your dreams will make you future oriented and give you a future ministry.

Dreams give hope and keep the spirit alive. One of the greatest things in life is hope. Hope has the power to prolong physical life. Hope has the power to bring a divided family back together again. Hope also has the power to keep you motivated on tough days or when you face a failure or when you don't have any answers to your problem. Hope will keep you looking until you find it.

Dreams can motivate you to grow spiritually. When you dream of doing something for God, you will be motivated to grow spiritually so you can accomplish those dreams. Just like dreams give hope to life and encourage physical growth, so do dreams encourage spiritual growth.

Chapter One Review

1. What is the first mandate of leaders?

2. What is the most powerful tool a leader possesses?

3. What are the four steps to becoming an effective leader and reaching your vision?

4. When setting goals, be sure to make SMART goals. What does the acrostic SMART stand for?

5. What four laws must you realize in order to make your dreams come true?

6. How can you keep your dreams alive?

Chapter Two

THE LAW OF REWARDS

Chapter Two

THE LAW OF REWARDS

The second law of leadership is the *law of rewards*. Simply stated, "The things that get rewarded get done." Zig Zigler puts it this way: "People will follow you where you want to go, if you help them get where they want to go." Christians want to walk with God, serve God, and experience the touch of God in their lives. If pastors give them what they want from God, the people will follow their pastor's leadership and help him build the great church that both pastor and people dream of building for God.

Law Two: The Law of Rewards	
Descriptive Statement	People follow a leader who provides them rewards from their self-chosen goals.
Prescriptive Statement	The leader must reward those who follow him.
Slogan	The things that get rewarded, get done.

Hindrances to Followers

A church accomplishes its ministry through its people. Therefore, pastors need to motivate laypeople to fulfill ministry goals. Pastoral leaders may encounter one or more problems hindering the progress of their ministries. Some need to learn principles of ministry to be effective and do things right. Others have a problem with priorities and are doing wrong things. Still others are doing things wrongly. Like the first group, those in this group need training in ministry principles. Then, there are some who are not doing things at all.

The challenge to the leader is to get each group moving in the same direction at the same time. As stated earlier, the things that get rewarded get done. How can everyone be properly motivated?

Assume you own a bottle-capping business and have five problem people working for you. The first is not doing things right. Even though you have a machine to put caps on bottles, this worker is putting caps on bottles manually and slowing the production line. The second is not doing right things. Instead of capping bottles, this person lets bottles pass by uncapped. The third person is doing wrong things. Instead of capping bottles, this worker spends time talking with others on the assembly line and may be better suited to work in the office as a receptionist. The fourth employee is doing things wrong. This person uses a hammer to cap bottles and often misses, breaking the bottle. The fifth problem employee is not doing any thing at all.

HINDRANCES
1. Not doing things right.
2. Not doing right things.
3. Doing wrong things.
4. Doing things wrongly.
5. Not doing things at all.

These problem employees are typical of many church members and represent the greatest problem in mobilizing the church for ministry. Therefore, church leaders must realize the law of rewards – the things that bring rewards from leaders get done. Great leaders understand what people want and see that their followers get what they want.

People do not usually do what you want them to do, what you dream of them doing, what you demand they do or what you punish for not doing. You can count on people doing things that benefit them the most. Therefore, do not reward the wrong activities.

Leaders must learn why people do what they do so they can reward them. People work for money, time off, affirmation, leisure, glory, promotion, rest, and love. In the church, people will work for the glory of God because God has worked in their hearts.

A good leader has leadership eyes, which are eyes to see the things that light fires in people's hearts and motivate them to become involved in a project. The "reward" principle will give you "leadership eyes." Do not look first for barriers, line of command or even the organizational flow chart. Look to see what is being rewarded. People who follow you behave according to what is being rewarded. The dynamics of your church organization is explained by the "reward" system.

Great leaders also understand the principles of leadership blindness. Followers are blinded to your direction, correction or education by their "reward system." They can only see what they do right or what rewards they get.

When a pastor released a youth pastor because over half the parents were opposed to his ministry, his response was to tell how many hours a week he worked and how many he had led to Christ. The youth pastor told all the things he had done right, because his personal reward system blinded him to his errors. Therefore, leaders need to communicate job expectations through a system of rewards.

Dr. John Maxwell, pastor of Skyline Wesleyan Church in greater San Diego, California, applies the law of rewards to the problem of American competitiveness in the international market. He asks, "Are American workers working at top efficiency?" The obvious answer is, "No!" The Japanese tend to be more efficient workers. Is the American work ethic dead? Again, the answer is, "No!" Americans love to work. Why then do they not work harder? The answer to this question is found in another question, "What is being rewarded?"

Generally, there is no relationship between quality of work and pay. American workers tend to be paid the same for adequacy as they are paid for excellence. Also, there is no relationship between quantity of work and pay. If workers in an automobile plant work faster and produce more cars, they do not see that increased production reflected in increased pay. Their job has become monotonous and impersonal, therefore, their pride is not tied to their job.

Is It Biblical to Reward?

Some denominations use awards to motivate their churches in ministry. They may award a plaque to the fastest-growing church in each association or the winner of a denomination-wide Sunday School campaign. They may recognize pastors who have led their churches through a building program in the past year. Pastors also may use awards to motivate church workers. Perhaps they should give an award to the outstanding Sunday School teacher of the year, the person who brings the most friends on Friend Day or an innovative worker who has developed a new and effective ministry in the church.

To manage people, leaders need to grab hold of the doctrine of sin. Everyone has a positive and negative pole. We all have our assets and liabilities. While this is especially true in the world, sometimes it is easy for a Christian leader to forget that Christians still have a sin nature. Every cloud has a bright and dark side. So it is also true of every Christian that they have been polluted by sin (Rom. 3:23), yet they also hold all the potential of one created "in the image of God" (Gen. 1:27).

The biblical basis of rewards is also suggested in the life and teaching of Jesus. He recognized the humanity of His disciples and appealed to self advancement (parable of talents), self worth (Matt. 22:39), and self protection (Luke 22:38; Rom. 13:4). In His doctrine of stewardship He taught the right of ownership, the dignity of work, the reward of labor, and the right of workers to anticipate advancement (Matt. 20:1-16; 25:14-30).

The Basis of Rewards

A good leader will give rewards to encourage his or her followers to work toward their dream. John Maxwell suggests the following list of things to reward. The first is faithfulness. Have you ever noticed how often people are commended for faithfulness in the Bible? When we reward faithfulness, we teach faithfulness. According to Comedian Woody Allen, "Eighty percent of life is showing up." By rewarding faithfulness, you encourage others to continue in their ministry for Christ and discourage them from quitting.

Leaders also need to reward innovation. Innovators have the hardest task in the church, but they also have one of the most important tasks in the church. Without innovation, churches do not enter new areas of ministry and growth. While the church should never change its message, it needs to constantly change its methods to remain effective and influential in a constantly changing world. In the parable of the talents, individuals were rewarded for creative thinking. Therefore, leaders should reward innovation and encourage innovative thinking.

Another area leaders should reward is solutions. There is usually more than one way to solve a problem. Those who come up with workable solutions to problems should be rewarded, to encourage others to look for solutions rather than problems in ministry.

Two people on a board or committee hold power. The first is the person who asks questions. This person has the power to stop progress. The second is the person who proposes solutions. This person has the power to move a group into new dimensions of ministry. Therefore, a leader must look for people who can answer questions with solutions. This helps the leader build confidence, ventilate negative feelings, lead the group to deal with solutions rather than emotions, and convince others he or she is not hiding facts.

Reward both thinking and action. Thinking is only the first step in problem solving. Action is the final step. Often, these represent two different people. One may come up with an idea, but another implements an action strategy to make that idea work. Both the person who came up with the idea and the one who made it work should be rewarded.

John Maxwell outlines several stages in resolving a problem when he states, "To look is one thing, to see what you look at is another, to understand what you see is a third, to learn from what you understand is still something else, but to act on what you learn is all that really matters."

Great leaders know how to reward both the simple and complex. The simple job done well is obvious to the masses. The complex job done well is obvious to the leader. The leader knows the success needed for both, and how to reward both and make each understand the other.

Leaders also need to reward both teamwork and individual excellence. None of us are as smart as all of us. Winning teams are led by great individuals, and winning individuals cannot do it without great teams. A wise leader will encourage cooperative effort and individual excellence by rewarding both.

There are several other things leaders should reward in their followers. Reward things like a positive attitude and loyalty to the church, the pastor, and one another. Also, reward personal growth. As people grow personally, their ministry for God grows. Another area which should be rewarded is people reproduction. As people reproduce themselves in others, their influence increases. Also reward creativity. There is no infinite cookie jar to fund ministry. Those who find creative ways to minister extend the life of their ministry.

Eleven Ways to Reward

There are several ways a leader can reward followers. Perhaps the most obvious is money: "The labourer is worthy of his hire" (Luke 10:7; 1 Tim. 5:18). Sometimes a pastor should consider rewarding a staff member with a salary increase or cash bonus. Money is what people work for. Avoid the two extreme attitudes of guiltiness and greediness when talking about money.

Staff can also be rewarded through recognition and praise, allowing them to share some of the glory for their work. A leader can build his or her followers and help them achieve their potential by praising them when appropriate. People are also rewarded with extra time off for a good job well done.

One of the creative ways some companies reward their employees is to let them buy stock in the company. Some companies have discovered that when employees hold share in the company for which they work, employee absenteeism goes down, production goes up, and the quality of the finished product is improved. In church, people are more committed to serve when they buy into the church and begin describing the church as "my church."

People can also be rewarded by letting them do the work they do best and enjoy most. Others are motivated to work when rewarded with a promotion or advancement in the company. Faithful workers can also be rewarded with greater freedom in a non-structured work environment. Some pastors reward their Sunday School teachers by giving them an opportunity to learn. They may give the teacher a book or pay the cost of their attending an area Sunday School convention. Another way to reward people is to include them in the decision-making process in areas related directly to them. This demonstrates the leader's increased confidence in that worker's ability.

Sometimes, the best way to reward others is through a special celebration. You may wish to take your staff to dinner or honor someone with a party. Other times, people should be rewarded with a gift or thoughtful action on the part of the leader.

Chapter Two Review

1. What does the Law of Rewards tell us?

2. What are hindrances to a progressive ministry?

3. There is a biblical basis of rewards. What are some examples taught by Jesus?

4. What should a leader reward in his or her followers?

5. What are some ways a leader can reward people?

Chapter Three

THE LAW OF CREDIBILITY

Chapter Three

THE LAW OF CREDIBILITY

The third law of leadership is the *law of credibility*. This law states that you must have a strategy that is accepted and believed by followers if you are to accomplish your goals. People will follow you when they trust you to get them to their goal.

First, leaders must have a dream to share with followers. That dream must be sharpened by objectives and include workable plans. Next, the followers must see the rewards they will receive for following the leader. The third step is establishing credibility. Followers must believe their leader's plan to give them the rewards of their dream. Leaders must follow these steps to secure the confidence of followers.

Law Three: The Law of Credibility	
Descriptive Statement	People follow a leader when they have confidence in his plans.
Prescriptive Statement	The leader must have a credibility plan to reach the objective.
Slogan	The leader who believes in his followers has people who believe in him.

A healthy group is going forward, reaching its goal, and experiencing positive interaction among members. Each member is growing because of his or her participation in the group. As members contribute to the group, their identification with the group makes a contribution to them. The Bible pictures this human relationship when it compares the church to a human body, "the whole body fitly joined together and compacted by that which every joint supplieth, according to the effectual working in the measure of every part, maketh increase of the body unto the edifying of itself in love" (Eph. 4:16).

Therefore, the group's secret of growth and success is the followers' attitude toward one another and toward the leader. A talented ball team may bicker among themselves and post a losing record. But after the manager is fired and a new leader is hired, everything is different. The new field leader fosters harmony and gets everyone to work together. Each player begins playing up to his potential and the team begins winning. What's the difference? A new attitude! A new winning spirit! They believe in themselves and in their leader.

The law of credibility means the leader must produce a winning spirit on his team. Teams with positive spirits win. Occasionally teams with lousy attitudes win, but only because of superior talent that enables them to climb over the barriers of bad attitude.

The leader is the key to healthy attitudes in a family, a committee, a policy-making board or the total church. As John Maxwell says, "The leader knows the way. Therefore, the leader needs knowledge. The leader goes the way. Therefore, the leader should have a deep commitment to Christ and the ministry. The leader shows the way. Therefore, the leader should also be the example to others."

THE LEADER
Knows the way.
Goes the way.
Shows the way.

In a typical building, two instruments make life comfortable for all, and in a real way contribute to how people function and get along with one another. The first is the thermometer which measures the temperature. It only tells us the warmth or coolness of the living environment. Second, the thermostat sets the temperature norm in the building. Leaders should not just be passive tools (thermometers) that only reflect conditions. Rather, leaders must be active tools (thermostats) that change the temperature.

Building Blocks to Lift Credibility

One of the primary concerns of a leader is to build personal credibility. People must believe in a leader before they will follow a leader. However, their belief is usually not absolute, but is measured on a scale of one to ten. They give their leader a little loyalty, say a "3" or "4," or they give him a lot of loyalty, a "7" or "9." Therefore, a leader must know the building blocks necessary to lift his followers' attitude to one another and to himself.

The first and absolutely necessary block to gain credibility involves being an example to your followers. A leader must do more than tell people where to go. He must go with them and show them the way. You may teach people what you know, but you reproduce only what you are. You model by example in several ways: attitude, appreciation, commitment, and enthusiasm. The way you choose a goal and your enthusiasm will influence your followers more than what you preach in sermons or write in interoffice memos. Your followers judge you by what they see, not by what they hear you say.

To teach others to "think right" is great, but to teach them to "do right" is better. It is also harder.

Enthusiasm is another building block that leaders use to build credibility in their leadership. Your enthusiasm is the first step in lighting fires in people's hearts and planting dreams in people's visions. Since enthusiasm is the fuel that keeps the fire going when you're not around, you have to give them your excitement for the dream.

How can a leader light fires in the hearts of his or her followers? Maxwell says there are four steps. (1) Express appreciation to your followers for who they are. (2) Share your anticipation of what you expect them to accomplish for God. (3) Recognize the accomplishments of your followers. Point out to them what they have already done or what others have done. (4) Be accountable for what you as the leader must do to get to the goal.

```
HOW TO LIGHT FIRES IN HEARTS
Express appreciation.
Share anticipation.
Recognize accomplishments.
Be accountable.
```

Build your followers' expectations. Be optimistic. Stretch their vision of what can be done for God. Help them dream. When you make people look up to your dream, they look up to your leadership.

How can you as a leader plant dreams in your followers? You must see the dream yourself. You must get your dream from God through prayer. It comes from the Word of God and its biblical principles. If your followers are believers, the dream will be reinforced in their times of prayer and Bible study. Tie your dreams to a verse of Scripture. When I went to Columbia (SC) Bible College as a freshman in 1950, the school motto was a dream in the heart of the college founder, Dr. R. C. McQuilkin, who wanted every student "to know Christ and make Him known." The president communicated that vision to students. We believed in it because we believed in him. We saw Christ in him and wanted the same walk with God that Dr. McQuilkin had.

A father leads a young family by a dream. He tells his wife and young children, "I'll get through college and begin a business. One day it will be a large business." The father's dream is a factory and employees. The mother's dream is living in a large executive mansion. The children see toys, a swimming pool, and their own car. The dream motivates the whole family to sacrifice to get Dad through college. They understand when he has to study each evening and spend Saturdays in the library. But the wife and family cannot dream, unless it first originates in the heart of the father as the leader.

After the leader sees the dream, he must share the dream with others. Maxwell says everyone deserves an opportunity to see a dream, even though not everyone will buy into it. People must at least see God and see what He can do. Your dream may be the only witness some will ever have of the glory of God or the truth of His revelation. Therefore, to be effective, the leader has an obligation to share his dream – to witness to all what God is doing in the world.

Another way to plant dreams is to build up your followers so they can see the dream and they see themselves capable of reaching the dream. When a leader convinces his followers, they can achieve the dream because they are actually better than they previously thought, the leader is on his way to success.

John Maxwell constantly says to "size" them higher than what they think they are. Most people will strive to live up to that expectation. Hence, the leader has "lit a fire" in their heart or "planted a dream" in their soul.

Maxwell says put a "ten" on everyone's forehead, even though many will only live at the "two" level. Many people will try to live up to your expectations regardless of whether those expectations are high or low. A mother who always tells her boys, "You are wonderful, brilliant children," will probably have sons who try to live up to her expectations. They will study and go the extra mile to please their mother. The opposite is also probably true. The mother who constantly tells her son how dumb he is will probably influence him accordingly. Perhaps he will not try to excel in school, simply giving in to the inevitable – "he is dumb."

Maxwell says he tries to see everyone with a "ten" on their forehead. If the leader honestly responds to them expecting the best, perhaps they will reach higher than they would otherwise.

Every child is born with great potential, even if he is physically or mentally endowed with only average ability. Usually, the adults around the child will determine if the child will rise above himself or will surrender control to the dark side of his nature.

Another way to communicate your dream with all followers is to share your dreams with winners. Losers usually won't accept the dream, which is another way of saying they won't accept your leadership. For losers, go back to the previous point...stretch them...size them higher than they are. If they stretch to your expectation, they stretch to your leadership. When a winner buys into your dream, they will share the dream with others, including other winners plus the losers.

According to the Praeto Principle (80/20), twenty percent of your people will be leaders and eighty percent of your crowd are followers. The dream will flow down from the twenty percent to other followers. The best generals spend time with the staff, not the troops. It is not wrong to spend time with followers, but a general can stretch himself only so thin. Therefore he communicates with his group winners and they communicate with the troops. So how does a leader build credibility among all his followers? Spend eighty percent of your time with the twenty percent of your followers who demonstrate the greatest potential for leadership. *When applied to the church, a pastor is not just a leader of people, he is a leader of leaders who in turn lead the people.*

When a team wins a victory, it builds credibility with followers. But the opposite is also true; a winning spirit leads to a victory. What comes first, the winning attitude among followers or the act of victory that gives a winning attitude to followers? Both feed off one another. Suppose a losing team has a losing attitude. How does a leader break the losing cycle and the losing attitude? John Maxwell says he must put some wins under the belts of his players. A good coach always schedules some easy exhibition games so his team can actually win. Perhaps this can turn around their losing attitude. A good leader wants his followers to achieve a positive winning spirit. Some say it does not matter whether you win or lose...until you lose. No one has fun losing. Winning is part of life.

Wins do several things for a team. Maxwell says that first, winning gives them confidence for the next game. When they think they can win, they play above themselves. Second, a few wins raises individual and team self-esteem. Those who know they can win are not likely to give up in a close game. Those who are not sure they can win probably never will. Third, winning increases energy. "Hope deferred maketh the heart sick: but when the desire cometh, it is a tree of life" (Prov. 13:12). Fourth, winning gains respect from others, including the opposition. A reputation for winning gives your team an edge in the mind of the other team. Finally, when a manager leads his team to win, dissension on the team ceases. A winning team usually is a harmonious team. They have to play together to win together.

WHAT WINNING DOES FOR A TEAM
Gives confidence for the next game.
Raises individual and team self-esteem.
Increases energy.
Gains respect from the opposition.
Produces harmony among members.

Friend Day is a church-growth campaign that helps pastors put some wins under the belts of their congregations. The pastor asks everyone to get their friends to sign a commitment card to come share Friend Day with them. As their friends sign the cards, the people begin to anticipate a good Friend Day because of the "wins" (the signatures they are getting). A church that has never felt like a winner suddenly feels like winning for God because they got their friends to commit to attending on Friend Day. Nationwide statistics reveal about fourteen percent of first-time visitors who attend on Friend Day will become a part of the church if each visitor is followed up correctly. Friend Day then becomes another win under the belt to convince the church it can effectively reach its community for Christ.

Leaders build credibility by equipping their followers to lead. The old Chinese proverb states that if you give a man a fish, he will eat today. But teach a man to fish, and he will eat for a lifetime. According to Maxwell, good leaders will equip their followers with the following five skills: *Attitude* – knowing how to feel about problems. *Creativity* – knowing how to think about problems. *Vision* – knowing how to look at problems. *Direction* – knowing how to begin to solve problems. *Ownership* – individuals taking responsibility to finish the problem-solving process.

FIVE SKILLS A LEADER MUST COMMUNICATE

Attitude: How to feel about problems.
Creativity: How to think about problems.
Vision: How to look at problems.
Direction: Where to begin to solve problems.
Ownership: Responsibility to finish solving problems.

A good leader will ask followers three questions as they equip their followers for action. (1) "What are your strengths?" (2) "What are your dreams?" and (3) "What windows of opportunity do you have?"

The first question will guide the leader to help each follower know his or her strengths (gifts) that will move everyone toward the goal.

The second question will help each follower examine his or her motives and dreams.

Finally, the third question will make followers aware of their opportunities for group action. Then the pastor can equip his people for leadership by encouraging them through developing their gifts, exposing them to other successful leaders, and giving them opportunities to use their gifts in ministry and leading others.

THREE QUESTIONS TO HELP FOCUS DIRECTION

What are your strengths?
What are your dreams?
What windows of opportunities do you have?

Leaders also build credibility by their ability to evaluate problems and make decisions. When leaders make good decisions they build credibility in their followers. People tend to overlook the bad decisions of fellow travellers because they are just following. Their bad decisions tend to hurt primarily the other fellow. In some cases bad decisions affect the whole team or the whole church. But a bad decision by a follower never hurts the team like a bad decision by the leader. One reason some followers are not leaders is that they do not have the ability to make good decisions. The role of the leader is to teach them how to make good decisions. But bad decisions by leaders have a far wider implication. Followers evaluate the bad decisions of leaders and lose confidence in them, then stop following them.

Leadership is like a pyramid. At the bottom, there is a breadth of latitude and freedom and people that will overlook mistakes. The farther up the pyramid you climb, the less room there is to maneuver and the less freedom there is to fail. When a young pastor begins his ministry in his first church, people are willing to overlook mistakes and be understanding of his youth. But as he matures and becomes a leader, they will tend to be less tolerant of his mistakes. Those who lead great ministries have a smaller margin of error than those who are fresh out of seminary or are pastoring smaller churches.

Wrap Up

Every pastor can become a better leader by building credibility among church members. A good leader will use all six strategies in this chapter to build credibility. He will be an example and positive leadership model before them. He will be enthusiastic and build fires in the hearts of his followers. Then he will build expectation among his followers and plant dreams in them. He will lead them into positive experiences that will put wins under their belts, convincing them they can win again. He will equip his followers to lead by putting tools in their hands.

Then he will make good decisions so his followers will continue to have confidence in his leadership ability.

SIX STRATEGIES TO BUILD CREDIBILITY

Be an example – a role-model to follow.
Express enthusiasm – build fires in their hearts.
Be optimistic – plant dreams in their spirits.
Lead into positive experience – put wins under their belts.
Equip with skills – put tools in their hands.
Make good decisions – build confidence.

Chapter Three Review

1. What does the Law of Credibility state?

2. What is the secret of a group's growth and success?

3. What are four steps to lighting fires in the hearts of followers?

4. What does winning do for a team?

5. What five skills will a good leader develop in his/her followers?

6. What three questions will help you focus direction?

7. What are six strategies to build credibility?

Chapter Four

THE LAW OF COMMUNICATION

Chapter Four

THE LAW OF COMMUNICATION

The fourth law of leadership is the *law of communication*. Leaders must communicate their goals and plans to followers if they are going to successfully lead them. Some leaders have difficulty getting others to follow because they have difficulty getting their ideas across to others. If people do not understand the leader, they will not follow the leader.

Law Four: The Law of Communication	
Descriptive Statement	People follow a leader who effectively communicates his plan to reach the objective.
Prescriptive Statement	The leader must effectively communicate his plans to reach the objective.
Slogan	People follow a leader who gives clear directions to his followers.

Communication is the act of exchanging information between individuals by a common system of signs, symbols or behavior. The key to effective communication involves using commonly understood language to communicate ideas.

John Maxwell says that since communication is a two-way street, the leader must be close enough to followers to get information to them and from them. The leader must also be close enough to God to get dreams and goals.

The leader must use language and gestures to effectively communicate to his or her followers. This means content must be effectively arranged and attractively presented.

Words often mean different things to different people. Sometimes Christian leaders hinder their leadership potential by using language which is not understood by those with a different background. While those raised in evangelical churches may appreciate the significance of words such as reconciliation, propitiation, and vicarious substitutionary atonement, these words are meaningless to the person without a similar church background. But one's religious background is not the only factor that colors the way we use language. The expression "catching a fly" means one thing to a baseball player, something entirely different to the boy with a hungry pet frog. Even the way one pronounces the word "bass" may depend upon whether that person is into music or fishing. The Oxford English Dictionary lists over one hundred different definitions for the word "run."

Good leaders understand that people use words to mean different things. Therefore, they are careful to use words that their followers understand.

Since communication is not a one-way street from the leader to his followers, there must be feedback. Followers must respond individually or corporately. Therefore, the leader should use words that are understood by the followers and the leader must understand the words used by the followers. When they understand each other, good communication occurs.

Great leaders are not always the best educated nor the least educated. Great leaders are those who know how to use the language of their people to communicate their ideas to their people.

The Process of Communication

The word communicate means to make something common to two people. A person communicating the command, "Give me a cold drink," has effectively communicated when the person to whom he or she is speaking gives the cold drink that is expected. Both the speaker (the person who encodes the message in words) and the hearer (the person who decodes the message) have understood the message.

There are four parts in the communication process. First, the sender-encoder (leader) must choose words with proper meaning to communicate an idea and must use the words properly. Second, the receiver-decoder (follower) must recognize and interpret the words to discern the message. Third, the message refers to the idea the leader attempts to communicate to the follower. Finally, the channel refers to the method the leader uses to communicate the idea to his followers.

The message originates in the mind of the leader. The leader chooses words that mean what he or she wants to convey to the followers. The message is placed in a channel to communicate to the followers. The followers receive the message and interpret it.

Problems in Communicating

As you consider the process of communication, you may notice several areas in which one might anticipate problems. One of these problem areas has already been alluded to – the different meanings of words. Leaders who have personal contact with their followers can usually tell when the followers have difficulty understanding the meaning of their words. When this happens, leaders should take the time to briefly explain the meaning of the word being used.

Some leaders hinder their communication by using big (polysyllabic) words when a smaller word may be better. Usually, leaders can choose between several words to express their idea. Generally the smaller, better understood word is best. When a larger technical term must occasionally be used, leaders should be careful to explain it, using simple words followers understand. As a leader, be careful of falling into the trap of equating using big words with being profound. In what may be the most philosophically profound passage in all of Scripture, the largest word is "beginning." "In the beginning God created the heaven and the earth" (Gen. 1:1). Yet philosophers have written volumes attempting to plumb the depth of meaning in this passage. The Bible was written for the masses rather than the intellectual elite; therefore, the Bible uses small words with big meanings. Likewise, biblical leaders should choose small, easy-to-understand words with proper meaning.

A third language problem in communication involves homophones; words which sound alike even though they have different meanings. The English words "heir" and "air" look different in print and have different meanings, but when pronounced, they may sound like the same word. Other examples of language problems are the English words "bare" and "bear" or the words "to," "too," and "two." When leaders use homophones, they should be careful to do so in a context in which a listener can quickly discern which word is being used and not be confused by assuming the wrong meaning.

The problem of homophones can be overcome easily in written communications. However, written communications can be hindered through the use of homographs which appear the same but come from different roots and have completely different meanings. In this book, the word "lead" is used in a context which suggests a meaning different than that which would be assumed if the same word appeared in a metallurgy textbook or a "how-to" book on electronic wiring.

Improper pronunciation and poor enunciation of words also hinder a leader's ability to communicate ideas. Pronunciation refers to emphasis on the proper syllable, using the correct short or long sound on vowels, and using the correct hard or soft sound on consonants. Enunciation means "to say every syllable distinctly." When a leader slurs his or her speech or pronounces words incorrectly, followers have difficulty following what is being said. Pronunciation is saying a word right, enunciation is saying a word clearly.

Good leaders communicate beyond the words themselves. They express ideas through body language and inflections in their voice. They speak with their smile, their hands or their eyes. When leaders fail to be expressive, they tend not to communicate as well as they might otherwise. When you as a leader speak to your followers, speak with an occasional exclamation mark. Also, do not be afraid to alter your volume up or down as appropriate or use the occasional gesture for emphasis.

Because communication is a two-way street, good leaders encourage followers to become involved in the process. They understand that followers remember more of what is communicated if they are actively involved in the process. Also, when followers speak, their words may reveal things about themselves which will help the leader lead better. Listen for where that follower is in his or her understanding of the goal or dream. Encouraging followers to be part of the communication process also helps leaders keep abreast of the constantly changing dialect of followers. As words come to have different meanings in common use, leaders will want to understand these new terms and their meanings. They will learn how to use them to become more effective communicators.

How to Communicate Your Ideas to Your Followers

According to the law of communication, leaders must function as communicators to be effective. In this role, leaders must know the message to be communicated, know which words are commonly used by followers, choose the specific words to use, choose the channel of communication, and relate their message through words.

Pastors enhance their leadership in church when they learn how to effectively communicate their ideas to their people. Most pastors know from experience that a simple pulpit or bulletin announcement rarely achieves its intended response. Good leaders tend to communicate an idea six to ten times before followers begin to grasp the idea and respond. Therefore, pastors should use a variety of means to communicate their ideas to their people.

Many pastors communicate with and lead their church through organized campaigns. If they want to communicate evangelism, they do so by conducting a church growth campaign. If they want to communicate stewardship, they do so through a stewardship campaign. If they want to communicate missions, they do so through a missionary convention.

The strength of leading people through an organized campaign is in the coordination of activities which communicate a single message. In a stewardship campaign, the pastor preaches on stewardship, church lay members give stewardship testimonies, various stewardship letters and tracts are sent to the church family, and Sunday School teachers explain principles of stewardship. By the time the pastor leads his people to make their stewardship commitment, they may have heard the intended message concerning their stewardship responsibility many times that month and are therefore prepared to make a commitment.

Pastors also apply the law of communication to lead their churches to grow when they plan a follow-up strategy based on the Law of Three Hearings and the Law of Seven Touches. Research suggests that the average person will attend a church three to four times before committing to the church. Therefore, when a person visits the church, the goal of the follow-up strategy is to get that visitor back a second and third time rather than only seeking an immediate commitment from the prospect. This is called the Law of Three Hearings because they will hear on three occasions before making a decision. Research indicates that people are most likely to return for a second and third visit if they are contacted by the church seven times the week following their first visit (the Law of Seven Touches). Therefore, the follow-up strategy coordinates letters, phone calls, and in-home visits so a person is "touched" by the church seven times. The leader uses workers, media, and a program to communicate his church's concern for the person.

Often, the actions of leaders are more effective than their words in communicating their ideas. In a stewardship campaign and carefully planned follow-up strategy, the leader communicates his or her message through both words and actions. This principle can also be applied to other church leadership responsibilities, including enlisting workers, planning calendars, budgeting resources, etc. As a leader becomes a more effective communicator, the improved communicator becomes a better leader.

Chapter Four Review

1. What does the Law of Communication mean?

2. What are the four parts in the communication process?

3. What things can cause problems in communicating?

4. What means can you use to communicate with your followers?

Chapter Five

THE LAW OF ACCOUNTABILITY

Chapter Five

THE LAW OF ACCOUNTABILITY

The fifth law of leadership is the *law of accountability*. People follow leaders who know where they are going. Most people want their leader to know them and their contribution to the movement. People want to be appreciated when they make a contribution to the team that moves them to the goal. But there is a flip side to this principle. It is the law of accountability. People do not always do what you expect them to do. They do what you the leader inspect. People will follow leaders who have a relationship to them. This relationship is both positive and negative. Leaders must reward and scrutinize people. Leaders who are only optimistic and not realistic about the failures and negative reactions of their followers will ultimately fail. Therefore, if you do not inspect, the people will not do what you expect.

Law Five: The Law of Accountability	
Descriptive Statement	People follow a leader who gives them responsibility to help reach the objective.
Prescriptive Statement	The leader must know the contribution that his followers make to help reach the goal.
Slogan	People don't do what you expect, but what you inspect.

A Sunday School superintendent is a leader of teachers. He or she can apply the law of accountability and lead the teachers to be better teachers. First, install a bell and ring it 15 minutes before Sunday School begins (when teachers should be in their classes). Ring it again when Sunday School begins (the whole Sunday School starts together), and ring it when the Sunday School ends (the whole Sunday School finishes together). Second, the superintendent can instill accountability by distributing a weekly teacher's report form that asks teachers to report when they arrived, how much time they spent in lesson preparation, how many teaching methods they used to teach, how many follow-up contacts they made with absentees, and how many contacts they made with prospects. When the teachers respond to their superintendent, they recognize his or her leadership over them and they display accountability to their task.

Good leaders lead people through job descriptions. A job description tells followers what is expected of them. Remember, they do not always do what is expected of them and usually will not do more than is expected of them. Needless to say, "expectations" is the baseline to the leadership-follower relationship. Some job descriptions are understood and no written statement is needed (what is expected of a father who leads the family). Others are communicated verbally and need no written statement (what passengers on a bus must do to have an enjoyable trip). Still others must be written for better performance (what a Sunday School teacher must do).

There are three things the people you lead want to know about their responsibility; therefore, their job description should answer three questions: (1) What am I to do? (2) What am I to accomplish? (3) To whom am I accountable?

There are several reasons why you should make your followers accountable.

Accountability implies the leader's partnership and help. A leader who holds his or her followers accountable, communicates the attitude that all of them are "in this thing together." There must be joint ownership.

Accountability will motivate followers to do a better job. Paul was motivated in his ministry by the awareness that he was accountable to God for what he did (1 Cor. 4:4).

Accountability gives the follower a basis of evaluation and a foundation upon which the leader and follower can work on problems together. An accountability tool like a job assessment survey can be used to communicate information, solve problems, and make decisions. Such a tool involves the followers in leadership.

Accountability serves as a tool by which leaders can realistically determine if they are succeeding.

Leadership holds others accountable for their responsibility, but ultimately takes responsibility for everything under it. Leadership must go beyond dreams and accept responsibility for the success or failure of the task.

Many pastors have great dreams in the work of God. They preach well and communicate their expectations. People know the dream, but the pastor does not follow through and the people do not follow. What happens to his wishes and hopes?

"If wishes and hopes were candy and nuts, pastors would have Christmas every day," says John Maxwell.

The Team Leader

Leadership is influence. The more people you influence, the greater your leadership. Leadership is never control. Pastors who exercise control over their church usually lead small churches.

Businessmen who control every detail of their business never allow the business to grow beyond their limitations. Parents who control every aspect of their children's growth into adulthood, hinder their children's growth and potential. A pastor, businessman or parent must influence and guide. Their success in this area determines their ultimate success.

Leadership is also plural. A successful church or business is never a one-man show. Leadership is not what you do to people. Rather, leadership is what you do with people. The shepherd leads sheep because he has a relationship with his sheep. A pastor leads his people because he has a relationship with them. A teacher leads his pupils because he has established a healthy relationship with them. A leader is not leading if there are no followers. He is just performing.

Leadership never exists in a vacuum. The Chinese have a saying that goes, "If you think you are leading and no one is following, you are just taking a walk." Therefore, leadership cannot exist independent of a group being led. Before looking at the eight laws of leadership individually, we must first understand the fundamental relationship between the leader and the group he or she leads.

Maxwell says there are several indicators of successful pastoral leadership. First, his ability to win and baptize people determines his influence. Second, his ability to build the membership and attendance determines his influence. Third, his ability to solve problems determines his influence. Fourth, his ability to make good decisions determines his influence. Fifth, his ability to raise money determines his influence. Considering these five factors, a pastor's ability to influence people to follow him determines the growth, success, and spirituality of the congregation.

The Team

Great leaders lead great teams. Since "greatness" is a relative measure, the success of the followers determines how great the leader is ranked. What makes a great team? The team must have a common goal. There must be an open line of communication. A crowd is not a team nor is an audience, they are just a group of people. The bigger the crowd, the larger the group of people. A team is a group of people who work together, walk together, and talk together about a common goal.

In the New Testament, the church is compared to a team in which each member of the team has different spiritual gifts contributing to the success of the entire team (Eph. 4:11-16). The church is not a business, rather, it is a body. Business "glue" is money and profits while body "glue" is relationships and attitudes.

Teamwork does two things for the team. First it improves results. Basketball coach John Wooden states, "It takes ten hands to put the ball through the hoop."

Wooden means the team scores points and wins the game when the team works together in its common goal.

Second, teamwork improves the players themselves. "Two are better than one; because they have a good reward for their labour. For if they fall, the one will lift up his fellow: but woe to him that is alone when he falleth, for he hath not another to help him up" (Eccl. 4:9-10).

According to John Maxwell, "The average church would grow if the people would just smile." By this he means that the real difference between strong churches and weak churches is usually the way they treat people; not that he believes all churches should be "positive-attitude" churches. A major sign of an effective leader is people who are happy with their church and its leadership. When leaders treat other members of the team in a positive way, they will contribute to the leadership. They will strengthen the church and become better Christians.

The team must grow. All growth involves change. All growth is change, but not all change is growth. Great leaders learn to effect change based upon what they want to accomplish – the dream they share with their followers.

Leadership is impacted by the principle of sowing and reaping. What a leader sows to his people is what grows in their hearts. The dream a leader sows in his congregation is where the people will look. The plans a pastor shares with his followers gives the direction to where the congregation will head. What the leader sows determines if his followers will work, sacrifice, and strive for the dream.

An old farmer understood the law of sowing and reaping. "If I always plant what I have always planted, I will always get what I have always got." Sowing and reaping determine a leader's success. If you always do what you have always done, you will always be where you have always been.

The leader also must remember the law of the seed. To get life from a seed it must be planted. Anything that is alive will automatically grow. The body grows by food (Bible) and exercise (ministry). The leader/pastor must both feed and lead his flock.

Growth begins on the inside and works its way out. A tree grows at the core, not the edge. So a church or any group of people grows with its leaders, not its adherents. Maxwell says, "to travel without, you must first travel within."

Teamwork

Four factors impact the effectiveness of teamwork. A team works together best when they have an element of trust in their relationship to one another. They know they can get more done by working together than by working separately. They are committed to affirming and appreciating one another, and there is a good manager or leader guiding them.

Teamwork begins with trust. Followers will grow, take risks, and be creative in their tasks if leaders trust them. Mistrust strangles initiative. Followers rebel at surprises or problems they cannot handle. Good communication from leaders to followers produces trust. "People are down on what they are not up on," explains Rick Warren, pastor of Saddleback Valley Community Church in Mission Viejo, California.

How can a leader build trust in himself and in the team? Predictability is a contributing factor. Others on the team need to know what to expect.

Leaders need to stand for those who stand for them. When a leader backs his or her followers, trust is communicated to them. Followers are not always right, but they have a right to know their leader is with them in their mistakes.

A leader who trusts others on the team will delegate to them. Non-delegation is non-trust.

Working teams also need a good economy of energy. Ten years ago, the average American had 26 hours of free time per week. Today people have 16 hours of free time per week. Therefore, people don't have as much time to become involved in ministry as they had even ten years ago.

Also, the increase in working women in society impacts a church's ministry. Today, 52 percent of American women work, up from 18 percent at the end of World War II. Then, most working women were single women who later gave up their jobs when they got married. Today, the working woman is most likely a working wife and a working mother or a single parent.

When college girls, older women and retired women are factored into the equation, about 80 percent of young and middle-age women are active in the work force today and do not have the time to give their churches as did previous generations. Leaders must accomplish more in ministry, with less time from followers. Leaders must economize the energy and time of their followers, then help them accomplish more.

Ministry can be compared to a flashlight battery. Just like every time a flashlight is turned on the battery is being drained, every new problem in the church drains energy from leadership. But Christ is the strength to recharge the battery (cf. Phil. 4:13).

Good leaders will lead their teams to work in energy cycles. This means using people when they have strength. Also, leaders must understand that pressures associated with sickness, changes, and financial problems drain the energy of the team.

Individual members of the team tend to work at different energy levels, at different times, for different motives. This is another reason to use people according to their usability.

Good leaders learn to measure results rather than activity of hours. They will emphasize time management for everyone on the team. Using people according to their usability means enlisting people to serve according to their unique spiritual giftedness. A person's spiritual gift gives that individual energy. Working outside their area of giftedness drains their energy.

Good leaders also affirm and appreciate the followers on the team. This builds the worker, builds the work, and builds working conditions and has a two-fold result. First, it honors God. Second, it makes recruitment an easier task.

Good leaders make work fun. Enjoying your work has become an American value. Make work enjoyable and meaningful. Make the task a positive chore, not a negative, draining task. The average person will sacrifice and go the extra mile for the things that make him or her happy – and will avoid that which is unpleasant.

What should a leader recognize and reward? Recognize *effort*. Those who attempt great things for God should be encouraged in their effort. Recognize *faithfulness*. Faithfulness is the most-often-mentioned subject rewarded by Christ in Scripture. Recognize *strengths*. Teach followers to build on their strengths. Recognize *ideas*. When everyone thinks alike, no one is thinking.

```
┌─────────────────────────────────────┐
│          WHAT TO RECOGNIZE          │
├─────────────────────────────────────┤
│          Recognize effort.          │
│       Recognize faithfulness.       │
│        Recognize strengths.         │
│          Recognize ideas.           │
└─────────────────────────────────────┘
```

There are a number of ways leaders can recognize their followers. Sometimes, leaders may recognize and applaud workers publicly, before others on the team.

Other times, leaders may elect to write a personal note to the worker and/or feature the worker in a newsletter article. Occasionally, leaders may present a special award or give the worker something specific as a reward.

The leader who builds others on the team needs a tool to discover growth in workers. Some pastors of churches with a large church staff use a weekly report card. Each week, staff members answer the following questions.

1.   I am making progress in the following areas...
2.   I am having difficulty in this area...
3.   I need a decision in this area...
4.   My goal before the next meeting is...

The weekly report card is one way to manage others on the leadership team. Good leaders become better as they learn management skills. They need first to learn how to manage *problems*. Some people believe good leaders never have problems. Actually, good leaders are good problem-solvers. Others view mistakes as reverses that merely teach us what does not work. Still others believe mistakes are to be punished. Good leaders realize that anyone who attempts something new is bound to make mistakes. They view mistakes as the tuition for an education. According to football coach Sam Rutigliano, "Football is a game of mistakes, and he who makes the fewest wins." The leader who makes the fewest mistakes and learns how to solve problems will be the most effective leader.

Great leaders stimulate the creativity of their followers. In the parable of the talents, creative solutions to problems were rewarded. Creativity in followers is an avenue to expanded ministry where funds are limited. Give team members permission to make decisions. Decisions are made by implementers. The farther down the decisions are made, the stronger the church.

Good leaders learn to overcome the barriers to communication. There are three common barriers which act like the walls of a pyramid to entomb leaders from their followers. The first is the belief that our way is the only way. Usually, there are many good ways to accomplish a task. Second, some leaders believe all people are the same. Actually, God has gifted every person differently and each is unique. Third, some leaders are blinded by the belief that everyone sees things as they do. But because every person is unique, each one may have a potentially unique perspective on the situation.

There are two doors by which the leader may escape his or her pyramid tomb and become a better leader. First, learn to ask questions. Asking the right questions will help you gather the data you need to make good leadership decisions. Second, learn to develop answer eyes. Baseball great "Yogi" Berra noted, "You can see a lot just by watching."

Great leaders rarely lead their people to vote. Rather they work within permission and support. When leaders call upon their teams to vote, they ask the teams to endorse an untried idea. Votes mean someone loses. A church that votes too often eventually has a congregation full of losers and morale is low. Low team morale impacts your leadership potential.

Chapter Five Review

1. What idea does the Law of Accountability convey?

2. What are the advantages of making your followers accountable?

3. What is leadership?

4.   What five factors indicate a successful pastor?

5.   What makes a great team? And what does teamwork accomplish?

6.   How can you discover growth in workers?

7.   What are barriers to proper communication and accountability?

Chapter Six

THE LAW OF MOTIVATION

Chapter Six

THE LAW OF MOTIVATION

The sixth law of leadership is the *law of motivation*. This law states that what a leader motivates, followers activate. To become a great leader, you need to learn how to light fires in the hearts of people and persuade them to work for God. The word "persuasion" is derived from two Latin words, *per* meaning through and *suazio* meaning sweetness. Persuasion means to sweetly lead others. When a leader applies the law of motivation, he or she gives followers a motive to work.

Law Six: The Law of Motivation	
Descriptive Statement	People follow a leader who gives them compelling reasons to reach the objective.
Prescriptive Statement	The leader must motivate followers to accomplish the objective.
Slogan	People follow you when you give them a reason to work.

Great leaders motivate their followers to rise above the average and sacrifice for the dream he or she has communicated to them. It is more than telling the dream or knowing what people want and directing them toward what they want. Great leaders motivate their followers to rise above mediocrity, to overcome insurmountable obstacles, to make the most of limited resources, and to come out of difficult circumstances. Why? So they can achieve the dream.

WHAT LEADERS MOTIVATE
To rise above mediocrity.
To overcome insurmountable obstacles.
To use limited resources.
To come out of difficult circumstances.

Leaders must motivate their followers to see the dream, therefore, leaders use all their resources to communicate the dream so everyone sees the objective as clearly as possible. The clearer they see the dream, the more they will work and live for the dream. This means motivation begins with the law of communication. Next, the followers must buy the dream. It must be their goal, not just their leader's goal. This means motivation begins with the law of accountability.

MOTIVATING BY THE DREAM
See the dream. Buy the dream. Own the dream. Share the dream.

The followers must own the dream after they buy it. Sacrificing to get the dream is one thing, while daily living the dream is another thing. Part of living out the dream is sharing it with others. In this whole process, leaders motivate the followers to buy into the dream, then own and live the dream. Finally, leaders motivate followers to share the dream.

The Seven Laws of Motivation

You can motivate your followers by applying the seven laws of motivation. These laws are principles by which you can "sweetly lead" people to do what you want them to do. Because people are unique and do different things out of different motives, some of these laws may be more effective with some people than with others. Good leaders will understand their followers and learn which laws tend to motivate which followers best. Then they apply each of the seven laws of motivation as required to successfully lead their followers.

The first law of motivation is the law of illustration. People usually identify with the people in the stories they hear and imagine they can experience the same results. Jesus was a great motivator and used the law of illustration when He told parables. As others listened to Him tell of a man working in the field or making a trip between Jerusalem and Jericho, they could identify with that character and imagine themselves doing the same thing. Then they were motivated to learn and change their behavior and lifestyle. If you want to be a good motivator, you have to learn to tell stories with which followers can identify.

The second law of motivation is the law of the bandwagon. People tend to hitch their wagon to a star. They want to be on the winning team or with the group that is going places. People follow trends or fads and buy what they think their friends are buying. They want to be "in" on the latest news or they want to buy the "hot" new product. Therefore, leaders must follow the first five laws of leadership to create a "bandwagon" mentality.

1. Have a goal that the people want.
2. Reward the people who strive for the goal.
3. Be a credible example of the goal.
4. Communicate the dream plan and tactics of reaching it to your followers.
5. Inspect where the people are and what they are doing to reach the goal.

When this happens, leaders create a bandwagon attitude among their followers that motivates people to greater loyalty.

Leaders reach turning points in ministry when they can begin to rely on followers to help them motivate others. When a youth pastor begins his ministry among a group of high school students, he may find himself standing alone in calling the group to live a godly life. But as young people begin to respond to his leadership, soon they begin inviting their peers to live a godly life. A pastor may be the only one in the church who is convinced that the church should adopt a particular outreach strategy, but as other members of the church become sold on the project, they will motivate the rest of the church to jump on the bandwagon and support the project. Good leaders will learn how to create momentum to motivate others to do the work of God.

The third law of motivation is the law of statistics. Most people will respond to your leadership when they realize how often an idea will work. Facts alone don't always motivate, but when they are applied and illustrated, they can move people to action. The law of statistics tells you the real situation and will motivate people to do something about it.

The fourth law of motivation is the law of the whip. Some of your followers will be motivated to a certain course of action primarily to escape the consequences or punishment of their current action. "The whip" is motivating people by fear or guilt. Spare the rod, spoil the child. There are times when followers need to be confronted with what is wrong and be rebuked. But biblical rebuke is never an end in itself. Rather, it is a means of motivating people to a correct response (cf. Titus 1:13). Leaders who are always down on their people abuse the law of motivation. When "the whip" is used extensively, leadership is actually hindered and the law begins to lose its effectiveness.

The fifth law of motivation is the law of soft soap – motivation by praise, recognition, a show of love or support. This law recognizes that some people tend to be more responsive when they are encouraged, rather than rebuked or ridiculed. This law of motivation needs to be used in moderation. If all a leader ever does is praise his or her followers, those followers will not be equipped to live in the real world where they are measured by negative expectations. Also, be careful when you use the law of soft soap. A leader can tell followers they are so wonderful that he or she exaggerates and stretches the truth. Remember, soap is composed of ninety percent lye.

The sixth law of motivation is the law of testimony. Most people respond to the confident leader who shares how he has successfully done what he asks others to do. An effective leader will testify before his or her followers to motivate them to go and do likewise.

The seventh law of motivation is the law of peer pressure. People usually follow the influence of others within their peer group or their support group. As an illustration, a teenager will usually do what other teens in his social circle are doing. Therefore, effective leaders learn how to use peer pressure to motivate group members who might otherwise impede the group's progress.

The Strategy of Motivation

The effective leader knows how to apply the seven laws of motivation to move his or her followers to action. Leaders must develop a strategy for motivation and apply these laws to a specific situation. Generally, there are six steps in applying motivation strategy.

First, you must know precisely what you are trying to accomplish. This is best expressed by a statement of goals. A goal is a dream with a deadline. Followers do not need a long speech or even a short speech from their leaders to be motivated. They simply need to know where their leader is taking them – where they are going together. In sports you must first know the goal of the game before you can score.

A boy wanted to play basketball, so his father, a pastor, purchased a backboard, goal, and net. He began setting it up in the backyard, but received an emergency call and had to leave before the job was complete. Everything was in place except the hoop and net. The father promised his son he would be back in two hours. The boy decided he would practice shooting at where the basket should be. He practiced his arch and release. But after five minutes he lost all motivation. There was just no success of making goals. Even though he shot the ball, he never scored. A successful score will motivate to continuous action.

A clear statement of a goal can motivate a nation to shoot for the moon. In the 1950s, the first important achievements in space were accomplished by the Russians. The American space program struggled to keep pace. But all that changed in the 1960s. In President John F. Kennedy's inaugural address to the nation, he gave NASA a goal. He said, "Before this decade is out, we will land a man on the moon." All the resources of the nation were mobilized to carry out that goal. President Kennedy made the speech in January 1961. On July 20, 1969, the first man in history stepped onto the lunar surface. That man was an American.

When using goals to motivate people, there are several steps a leader must take to prepare them to make a decision. Leaders must consider what response is needed to accomplish the goal and know what they want their followers to do before they can convince them that the goal can be accomplished. Leaders must be concerned about what to say to get the job done, possess a sense of conviction about what needs to be done, and be able to propose a series of action steps to help followers begin moving toward the goal.

STEPS TO HELP PEOPLE ARRIVE AT A DECISION
Know what people must do.
Know what to say to them.
Be convicted that they will do it.
Propose a series of steps to the goal.

These four steps explain the way a pastor motivates his church to bring friends on Friend Day. First, he considers the needed response and tells his people, "I want you to bring your friends on Friend Day." Then he establishes credibility by reading a letter from the mayor who has agreed to come as his friend. He explains step by step what needs to be done to accomplish the goal. He communicates his conviction about winning friends to Christ as he preaches on friendship during the campaign. Finally, he gives people in church the opportunity to get their friends committed to attending with them on Friend Day.

A leader can motivate people by putting himself/herself in the other person's shoes. To help the leader understand his or her followers, there are several questions that need answers.

What do they know? To motivate people, you must start where people are. Preachers usually are content centered. Communicators usually are listener centered. What they know will color their perspective. If all a person has is a fork, everything looks like a meal.

What do they feel? Many people will respond to your leadership emotionally. If they are frustrated, they will not think with their heads. Most people respond from their heart. Ralph Waldo Emerson illustrates this in a story about a farmer who tried to get a calf into a barn. A storm was coming that would endanger the safety of the animal, but when the farmer and his son tried to drag the calf into the barn, it resisted. When they tried to lift it, it was too heavy. Then the farmer's daughter appeared in the field and put her sugar-coated finger into the calf's mouth. As she continued dipping her finger in a pocket full of sugar and offering it to the calf, the calf willingly followed her into the barn.

People go where they get the sugar they seek in life.

When Michael Faraday invented the electric motor, there seemed to be few businessmen who saw the potential of the new invention. Eventually, Faraday presented the idea to the Prime Minister of England hoping to win support. When the Prime Minister saw it, he asked Faraday what good the motor was. Faraday explained that the motor could help produce products that could be taxed and add to the government's income. He won the support of the Prime Minister by appealing to the politician's instinct to raise taxes, not by describing the benefits of his invention.

What do they want? This question helps you identify expectations. Remember, "You can get everything you want in life if you help other people get what they want."

Every year Americans purchase exercise equipment to lose weight. They do not put out money, sweat, and groan because they believe being overweight is harmful, but because they have a dream of being thin. When a business offers people what they want (equipment to help them become thin) people give them what business wants (sales).

When leaders begin looking at things from their followers' perspective, they can better motivate them to accomplish what they want.

John Maxwell tells the story of the most successful real estate agent in the Los Angeles area. He is a blind man. Someone asked how he, a blind man, could sell so many homes. He explained that when a couple came into his office looking for a home, he gave them the book of current real estate listings and asked them to find something they liked. Then as he rode to the home with the couple, he asked them to describe the neighborhood to him. At the home itself, he asked the people to describe each room to him. He summarized his successful sales strategy in the statement, "I sell through the other person's eyes."

A leader can motivate people to accomplish the dreams they seek in their heart.

Fourth, expose and address major problems before followers raise them as barriers or obstacles. Successful leaders expose problems and answer them first, knowing that if their followers raise the problems, they will not move to the goal. They will give up or refuse to follow. John Maxwell illustrates this by referring to the 1960 presidential elections. John F. Kennedy realized a major problem could keep him out of the White House. He was an Irish Catholic and America had never elected a Catholic as president. America was predominantly a protestant nation and had a significant anti-Catholic sentiment. Kennedy raised the issue and dealt with it by arranging a meeting with about 500 Southern Baptist pastors in Houston, Texas. Southern Baptists were considered one of the more conservative groups in the nation. When they agreed that Kennedy's religion alone should not stand in the way of his holding public office, the Catholic issue never became a significant barrier to his campaign.

According to Maxwell, there are several reasons why you as a leader should address problems. If you do not raise the issue first, others will think you are hiding something. Second, not dealing directly with the problem will color the issue in the thinking of followers. Third, existing problems will keep people from dealing with the issues. They will be problem-oriented rather than issue-oriented. Fourth, problems tend to raise barriers and create negative feelings directed toward leaders. Therefore, when leaders address the problem that everyone is aware of, people gain confidence in their leadership.

A fifth step in motivating people involves calling for a commitment. Be prepared to ask people to sign on the bottom line. As a leader, you need to be intentional because you will meet strong levels of resistance. Therefore, be prepared to win some votes and lose others. Successful leaders win more than they lose. Then they forget about the losses, only retaining the lessons they learned. Evangelism works when you help people see their need and extend an invitation to accept Christ. Some will accept; some will not. Therefore, be a leader and take the risk involved in asking people for a decision.

Leaders should be willing to take risks when they are committed to their dream and they are ready to take steps to accomplish their vision. The success of the civil rights movement was largely due to the risk-takers who believed in their cause and were willing to risk the abuses of police beatings, fire hose dousings, and dog attacks. When America saw that these committed leaders of the civil rights movement were enduring, they finally realized that people should not be treated that way and began to support their cause. The movement gained momentum and laws were passed because a few leaders had a dream and were willing to place themselves at risk to accomplish their dream.

This brings us to the sixth motivating step: appeal to the higher vision of your followers. Those who are successful in marketing see the higher dream. Maxwell states that these marketers know people don't buy newspapers; they buy news. Ladies don't buy cold cream; they buy beauty. Teens don't buy records; they buy excitement. This principle can also be applied beyond sales and business. For instance, students don't love studying; they study to have success in life.

Chapter Six Review

1. What does the Law of Motivation state?

2. What will great leaders motivate people to do?

3. What are the seven laws of motivation?

4. What are six steps to applying motivation strategy?

5. Why should leaders address problems?

Chapter Seven

THE LAW OF
PROBLEM-SOLVING

Chapter Seven

THE LAW OF PROBLEM-SOLVING

The seventh law of leadership is the *law of problem-solving*. Good leaders solve the problems that hinder people from reaching their goals. They understand that problems do not mean their work is unusual, unspiritual or unique. Rather, they view life as a game of errors and understand that those who solve the problems get ahead.

Law Seven: The Law of Problem-Solving	
Descriptive Statement	People follow a leader who gives solutions to problems that hinder them from reaching the objective.
Prescriptive Statement	The leader must solve problems that hinder followers from reaching their objective.
Slogan	The more barriers that frustrate your followers, the less likely they are to reach the goal.

How do you respond to problems? When things begin to fall apart, people have a tendency to ask three questions. Why me? Why now? Why this? When we ask these questions, we tend to do so as though it is God's or somebody else's fault that we are in our present mess. Often, our problems are simply the natural consequence of a previous action and there is no one to blame. Problems are simply the consequences of life.

THREE COMMON QUESTIONS
1. Why me?
2. Why now?
3. Why this?

Leaders need to know three things about problems. First, you cannot run from problems. Your world will never be problem free because you live in a fallen world, inhabited by fallen people. Second, you cannot stop problems from happening.

Those who believe Christians or ministers are exempt from problems are disillusioned. The greatest leaders in the Bible had problems. Third, problems can be solved. Solving problems is the path to growth. Your growth as a Christian or as a leader is directly related to your ability to handle problems. Success in life is not living without problems, but rather learning how to solve problems and keep moving ahead.

Developing Problem-Solving Skills

Those who aspire to be good leaders need to develop skills to handle problems. They need the ability to predict when and where problems will arise. As a college administrator, I recognize that the first week of November is the toughest week in the school year. This is the week that problems are most likely to arise in the life of college students. This is the greatest week of dropouts. Many pastors discover that their people tend to become easily discouraged about mid-February. If you live in a highly mobile suburban community, you may lose several of your key workers as they move during the summer months. Professional boxer Joe Lewis said, "The hit that knocks you out is not the hardest, but the one you do not see coming." Therefore, knowing when to expect problems will help you face them and solve them rather than be surprised and defeated by them.

Leaders need personal confidence in their ability to solve problems. As leaders solve small problems, they become confident to solve larger problems. The church moves forward from victory to victory. Some pastors may find it helpful to keep a list of problems they have solved. This will develop confidence they need to face and deal with new problems.

This practice also helps leaders expect victory out of solved problems. Too often, a problem threatens the success or momentum of a project. Good leaders know that solving the problem may actually help boost momentum and morale. Solving a small problem may contribute to an ultimate victory in the larger task. Look at problems as something to conquer rather than something that makes you want to quit.

What Causes Problems?

As previously noted, you will never escape your problems. While you may be able to avoid some problems in life or minimize their effect on you, you will always have problems. They are a natural part of life and cannot be eliminated completely.

THREE CAUSES OF PROBLEMS
1.   Change
2.   Differences
3.   Circumstances

Problems are caused by change. Christians do not like to change. Therefore, when you change the church program, you invite problems. But when churches grow, they change. Therefore, growing churches have problems. The growing church in Acts encountered problems. When churches go, there is motion. When there is motion, there is also friction which leads to breakdown and more problems. The Duke of Cambridge once gave a quotation that reflects many churches, "any change for any reason, for any purpose, should be deplored." A growing leader cannot afford to adopt that attitude.

Differences also cause problems. As a church grows, it begins to reach people from different backgrounds who hold different values from those who have been raised in the church. Often those reached by a growing church have different dreams for the church than those who have been a part of the congregation for a longer period. Each of these differences is a breeding ground for problems. The question is not *if* these differences will cause problems, but rather when and where these differences will arise.

Another cause of problems in a growing church is circumstances. A church may want to buy land to relocate and encounter problems in the form of city zoning ordinances. A local industry employing a significant number of church members may have an extended strike, announce a large lay-off or relocate to Mexico. Perhaps the annual Christmas parade is rerouted by your church and roads are closed so that people cannot get to church for worship. When you encounter a circumstance which you cannot control, you need to recognize it as a fact of life and move on. If you can do something about the circumstance, then face it and solve it.

How to Solve Your Problems

To begin your problem-solving process, learn to ask the following questions.

THREE QUESTIONS LEADERS ASK
1. How big is the problem?
2. Who is involved in the problem?
3. What do the followers think about the problem?

How big is the problem? Often a problem seems larger than life when it first arises and surprises you. Determine the basic issue involved in this problem. Are these issues significant enough to dwell on?

Consider who is involved in this problem. In any given church, there are some individuals who always seem to alert the pastor to minor problems, yet describe the problems in such a way as to suggest they are much larger than they really are.

Discern the motives involved in the dispute. Most problems are a conflict of attitudes rather than a dispute over things.

Determine the best time to address the problem. Many problems will work themselves out, without your involvement, if given time. Other problems need to be given time to let emotions cool or allow issues to come into focus before you attempt to resolve them.

What do the people most directly involved in the problem think? Get them together or consult them individually to gather data. Poll them to determine the facts, discover attitudes, and gain insight into the nature and timing of this problem. When you consult those most directly involved in the problem and encourage their input, you will strengthen your ability to lead these people as you resolve the problem.

What does the rest of the church think about the problem? Most problems in a church will affect one segment of the congregation directly, but may involve other parts of the congregation indirectly. Therefore, seek the input of others in the church to help you understand the problem and develop a solution. People only ask advice from those they respect. When a pastor consults others in the problem-solving process, he is telling his people he respects them and their contribution to the life of the church. When this happens, they will respond with greater respect for his leadership.

There are six common attitudes toward problems that arise in the church. These attitudes are:

1. To launch an all-out war over the problem.
2. To attack the problem.
3. To fuss over a problem and treat it like an irritation.
4. To feel threatened by the problem and surrender.
5. To retreat and suppress the problem.
6. To apply a strategy to solve the problem.

Ultimately the best course of action is applying a strategy to *solve* the problem. A wise leader needs to learn to discern the seriousness of a problem and decide how to deal with it.

Also, good leaders pick their own battles. Be careful not to let someone else choose your battles. There is always a cause that will motivate some people to battle (i.e., abortion, civil rights violations, the sale of alcohol or pornography, etc.). The leader needs to choose the battles about which he or she personally feels strongly and develop a winning strategy. The leader who always fights every dragon, will eventually lose his or her credibility as a leader.

THREE PROBLEM-SOLVING EYES
1. Eyes to see the positive.
2. Eyes to see the people.
3. Eyes to see the facts.

Leaders who solve problems develop "problem-solving eyes" to see the positive in the problem, to see the person who causes problems, and to see the facts relevant to the problem. Emotional eyes are blinded with tears. Fearful eyes are blinded with terror. Problem-solving eyes are focused on the problem to gain a better understanding of the problem and how to solve it.

Problems grow when you lose perspective, surrender your values, feel sorry for yourself or blame others. Therefore, a leader must have a positive attitude toward negative problems. The leader cannot give up nor can he or she give in to problems. Since problems are inevitable, they must be solved.

Perhaps the circumstances from which you long to be free are actually the circumstances being allowed by God to make you what you long to be.

As you look for a handle on solving your problem, begin at the scriptural solution to the problem. Take time to write out the scriptural principles by which you live. Ask, "How have others in Scripture solved a similar problem?" Answering this question will drive you to read the Bible and learn from others. As you see how others overcame similar problems in Scripture, you will discover biblical solutions which may be applicable to your situation. Strive to keep a balance between the Word (head knowledge) and the Spirit (heart expression) as you address the problem. Too much spirit without the Word will lead to an emotional blow up. Too much Word without the Spirit will cause you to dry up. But the right balance of the Word and Spirit will lead you to grow up.

Usually, there are several ways a problem can be resolved. It is up to the leader to chose one way and commit himself or herself to that answer. There is an inherent power in a decision. People who have difficulty deciding what to do often have this problem because they have a fear of failure, think the problem will solve itself, are insecure in their choices or have not surrendered to God. Do not let anything hinder your leadership ability to decide on the solution to your problems. You will never have the power to obey God until you first make the choice to obey.

Once you have decided on a solution, make it work. Declare your decision openly before your followers. Use various means to communicate your plan to others as you lead them to overcome the problem. In summary, when you encounter problems, gather the facts, define your objectives, make a decision, then make it work.

When you do a good job of solving problems, you will become a better leader. Check your decision-making process by the following results. When you solve problems, your people will have a higher level of morale, deeper confidence in your leadership, and incentive to fulfill the mission of your church.

If you want to be a better leader, develop your problem-solving skills and become known as one who can solve problems.

Chapter Seven Review

1. What thought is the Law of Problem-Solving based on?

2. What do people commonly ask when things begin to "fall apart"?

3.   What causes problems?

4.   How can you begin to solve problems?

5.   What are six common attitudes toward problems?

6.   What do "problem-solving" eyes see?

Chapter Eight

THE LAW OF
DECISION-MAKING

Chapter Eight

THE LAW OF DECISION-MAKING

The eighth law of leadership is the *law of decision-making*. Good leaders must constantly make good decisions. Everyone makes decisions every day of their life. People are where they are today because of decisions they made in the past. Their present decisions determine what kind of people they will become in the future. Great leaders make great decisions and accomplish great feats. Average leaders make average decisions and have a maintenance tenure. Poor leaders make poor decisions that hurt the cause and harm their followers. The law of decision-making may be the most important, yet most difficult, law of leadership to learn and consistently apply.

Law Eight: The Law of Decision-Making	
Descriptive Statement	People follow a leader who gives answers to the decisions involving their objective.
Prescriptive Statement	The leader must make good decisions that move followers toward the objective.
Slogan	Leaders make good decisions on good information, bad decisions on bad information, and lucky decisions on no information.

The president of a successful bank gained a reputation for his business skills. He had developed the bank from a small building on the corner in a little town, to become the tallest building in the core of a large city that grew from the suburbs surrounding his town. On the day of his retirement, this bank president was cleaning out his desk when a younger vice-president came to his office.

"How did you become so successful in banking," the young man asked.

The elderly banker stopped putting things in his briefcase and thought for a minute. Then he answered in two words, "Good decisions."

The young man pondered the answer, then asked, "How did you learn to make good decisions?"

The elderly man came around from behind his desk and responded with one word, "Experience."

The younger banker was persistent because he wanted to learn the secret to success in his chosen profession. "And how do you get experience?" he asked.

The elder banker began smiling to himself as he reflected on his years of banking. He answered the question with two words, "Bad decisions."

The law of decision-making is closely related to the law of problem-solving. Problems force leaders to make decisions. Decisions help leaders solve problems. When leaders make bad decisions, they should learn from that experience what will not work. That experience then helps them make better decisions in the future.

How Leaders Are Hindered from Making Good Decisions

There are several factors which may hinder a leader in making good decisions. A leader's decision-making may be impacted by a perception of what is expected, a previous commitment, other principles by which the leader lives, and the quality of information upon which the decision is made.

Several ministers went into a restaurant and surveyed the menu before ordering. Each was reluctant to decide until the pastor of the largest church ordered, in their opinion, the worst item on the menu – quiche with a side order of broccoli. The others followed the first minister's example and ordered the same. As the waitress was about to leave, the first minister called to her, "I've changed my mind. I'll have a cheeseburger and french fries instead." There is too much of this "follow-the-leader" mentality in decision-making.

Sometimes a leader will be reluctant to make a decision and does what he or she believes is *expected* in that situation. A pastor may lead his church into a building program and opt to use a certain builder because the last six churches that built in his denomination used that builder, not because that company is best. A director of Christian education may survey the various Vacation Bible School curricula published each year but consistently choose the same publisher because it is the same publisher that produces the church Sunday School curriculum, not because it is the best for the church.

Previous decisions impact future decisions. If a customer is being entertained by a salesperson, his previous decision to lose weight may cause him to pass on the rich dessert offered with the meal. Likewise when a pastor makes a decision about the general direction of the ministry for the year, he eliminates the need to make hundreds of other decisions concerning special offers available to the church. If a music director decides to purchase a new synthesizer, the offer of a discount on a used pipe organ should not be sufficient enticement to change that decision.

Other principles by which a leader lives will also impact his or her decisions. If a leader never makes impulse decisions as a matter of practice, then his or her response is always "no" to a high pressure salesman who has "the opportunity of a lifetime." Likewise, if a leader appeals to a board of advisors before making major decisions, then a decision will not be made until the leader has had opportunity to meet with the advisors.

The leader's ability to make good decisions is also related to his or her grasp of the facts in a situation. You cannot make good decisions on bad facts. You make bad decisions on bad facts. Also, you cannot make good decisions on no facts. If you happen to make a good decision without the facts, you call it "lucky." You make good decisions on good information.

How Decisions Are Made

Leaders need to know the five steps in the decision-making process in order to make good decisions.

First, leaders must be aware of a problem or question that needs a decision. They must realize that something is wrong, a new need has arisen, something can or should be improved, a new idea is advanced or a superior has made a request. Decision-making begins with the realization that a decision needs to be made.

Second, leaders need to take time to define the problem, issue or question. Sometimes the apparent problem is only a symptom of a greater problem. When the disciples in the early church in Jerusalem complained about the way for which widows were cared, the apostles realized an ethnic tension was the real problem and the care of widows was only a symptom. Therefore, they appointed seven Hellenists (Greeks) to be responsible for caring for widows (the symptom) and in doing so relieved ethnic tensions (the real problem) in the predominately Jewish church (Acts 6:1-7).

The third step in decision-making involves an analysis of the problem. Leaders should gather facts, determine causes, redefine the problems, evaluate assumptions, develop alternatives, and evaluate those alternatives. This may be the most involved step in the decision-making process because it involves interpreting the issue about which a decision must be made and considering all possible decisions which should be made. Only then should the decision itself be made.

The fourth step is making the actual decision. To make a decision before a need has been recognized, defined, and analyzed will probably mean the decision is not as good as it might otherwise be. Good leaders refuse to take this fourth step until they are assured the previous three steps in the process have been taken. Then they make their decision based upon what they learned in the previous steps.

The fifth and final step in the process is action. When a decision is made, leaders need to propose an implementation strategy to insure the need is addressed. This step involves the participation of those affected, communication between the leader and his or her followers, follow-up consultations during the implementation period, and periodic evaluations of the results.

FIVE STEPS IN DECISION-MAKING

Face the problem
Define the problem.
Get as much information as possible.
Choose a solution.
Make the decision work.

How to Make Better Decisions

Every leader should have a decision-making strategy to make good decisions. In many churches, the church constitution or bylaws may have certain requirements as to how decisions are made in that church. Pastors should consider those requirements as they lead the church in decision-making. If they cannot work properly within the guidelines, the leader should work to amend the bylaws or constitution. Regardless of the unique requirements of his church, every pastor should follow several steps to make better decisions.

Look to God for His wisdom through prayer and studying Scripture. God gives wisdom in great abundance to those who request it in prayer (James 1:5). Many Christians pray only when they are in trouble, but they could avoid many of these crises if they would pray about everything, especially for the daily guidance of God as they make decisions about every area of their life. Also, wisdom is gained through studying Scripture (2 Tim. 3:15). As you study Scripture, you will gain a better grasp of the principles of the Word of God which in turn will give you the tools you need to make the right decisions.

Discuss the issue with others you respect and who know you. Before making a decision that will impact your family, husbands should discuss it with their wives. "A prudent wife is from the Lord" (Prov. 19:14). Often, husbands and wives have unique differences which are complementary to each other in the decision-making process. Pastors should discuss major decisions impacting the church with other church leaders (members of the pastoral staff, church board, heads of ministries, etc.). Again, God often places different types of people in leadership positions in a church to complement each other in the decision-making process. Seek input from others who will be impacted most directly by your decision. Before making a major decision about Sunday School, the pastor should consult the Sunday School superintendent and other Sunday School workers for their input. Many church members understand the concept of team leadership or shared leadership in their place of business and expect church leaders to lead by this same approach. Shared leadership involves many in the decision-making process. This way the leader gives his followers the limits and strategy of the decision, but he allows them to make it with his or her guidance. This way the followers: (1) may offer practical suggestions for implementing decisions that might be overlooked by others less familiar with the actual situation, (2) may come up with creative alternatives that would accomplish the objective better, and (3) are more likely to support the final decision if they had a part in the process.

Of course, you will not accept all the advice you receive from others with the same level of credibility. "The simple believeth every word: but the prudent man looketh well to his going" (Prov. 14:15). When you consult others for their advice, you reserve the right to make your own decision. God ultimately holds each of us, not our advisors, responsible for our own decisions (cf. Matt. 25:14-29).

Consider various alternatives before deciding on a specific course of action. Usually, there is more than one good decision that can be made in response to a question, issue or problem. A good leader will carefully consider each option before coming to a conclusion. List each option on a separate sheet of paper and list the assets and liabilities associated with each decision in two columns on the page. Few leadership decisions involve all assets with no liabilities. Be careful not to look for what you want to see, but objectively evaluate each alternative on its own merits. Then the final decision will be stronger and you will know not only why you chose that course of action, but also why you did not choose another alternative.

Take as much time as you need to make the best decision. Do not be in a hurry to respond to an urgent situation if giving it time will help you get a better view of the problem or gather more facts. I heard John Maxwell say, the wrong decision at the wrong time is a disaster. The wrong decision at the right time is a mistake. The right decision at the wrong time is not acceptable. But the right decision at the right time leads to success. Therefore, make right decisions, but make them at the right time.

THE MAXWELL RULE OF DECISION-MAKING

1. The wrong decision at the wrong time is a disaster.
2. The wrong decision at the right time is a mistake.
3. The right decision at the wrong time is not acceptable.
4. The right decision at the right time leads to success.

Also, think through the consequences of your decisions before implementing them. Many decisions are made in the flesh, and are reflected on the short side of the ledger sheet. Do not use "stopwatch" thinking in making a decision. Rather, use "calendar" long-range reflection and consider the consequences of your decisions.

The first way to think through the consequences is to ask, "How will it affect me?" Ask how will it affect you physically, spiritually, socially, but most of all how will it affect your family? A father got a promotion and large raise. He moved his family to another state, but could not find a biblical church. Previously, they had been growing in the Lord and serving Christ. Now they became backslidden. There was no support of a good church. His made a decision based on the financial results, but did not make it in light of the total consequences for him and his family. Before a father makes a move concerning his job, home or even vacation, he needs to ask how it will affect his family.

Lot moved to the well-watered plains of Sodom and Gomorrah because it was the best place in the area (Gen. 13:10-11). However, his decision destroyed his children and he lost his wife. He made a wrong decision and lost everything. Even though Lot eventually got out of Sodom with his life, there were eternal consequences for his family.

Expect God to confirm your decision. Talk to God's people and ask them what they think about your decision. Pray with them. When you have to make a major decision, consult other spiritual leaders. Tell them where you are in your walk with God and ask them to help evaluate your decision. Paul referred to "the peace of God, which passeth all understanding, will guard your hearts and minds through Christ Jesus" (Phil. 4:7). The peace of God is like an umpire in a ball game. Normally, both the batter and pitcher are agreed whether a pitch is a strike or a ball, but in close calls both must accept the call of the umpire. When you make decisions, the value of those decisions should be readily apparent to yourself and perhaps others by the time you are ready to announce that decision. On the comparatively rare occasions when they are not, the inner peace of God may confirm your decision (if it is present) or prompt you to consider another course of action (if it is absent).

Finally, when you make a decision, make it work. A good leader can make a second- or third-rate decision work if he or she is fully committed to it, but a leader who is not strongly committed to making the best decision work may experience failure. "A double-minded man (is) unstable in all his ways" (James 1:8). Leaders who constantly change previous decisions eventually lose their credibility as leaders and people stop following. Take all the time you need to weigh the various options before making your decision. Then, once the decision has been made, support it and do what is necessary to make that decision work.

Chapter Eight Review

1. What does the Law of Decision-Making tell us?

2. What factors hinder a leader from making good decisions?

3. What are the steps in decision-making?

4. How can you make better decisions?

Appendix

DEFINITIVE STATEMENTS ON LEADERSHIP

General Statements

Leadership is a process in which an individual or group of individuals take initiative to assist a group to move toward production goals that are acceptable, to maintain the group, to dispose of those needs of individuals within the group that impelled them to join it, and to innovate.

  – Harold W. Boles & James A. Davenport

(1) One who walks ahead of the group; (2) Keeps in advance without being too detached; (3) Influences followers and moves them toward goals.

  – Charles L. Chaney & Ron S. Lewis

The exercise by a member of a group of certain qualities, character and ability which at any given time will result in his changing group behavior in the direction of mutually acceptable goals.

  – Kenneth Gangel

Leadership is the capacity and will to rally men and women to a common purpose, and the character which inspires confidence.

  – Lord Montgomery

A leader is a man who knows the road, who can keep ahead, and who pulls others after him.

  – John R. Mott

Leadership may be defined as that quality in a leader that inspires sufficient confidence in his subordinates as to be willing to accept his views and carry out his commands.

  – Fleet Admiral Nimitz

Leadership is influence, the ability of one person to influence others. One man can lead others only to the extent that he can influence them to follow his lead.

　　– J. Oswald Sanders

The activity of influencing people to cooperate toward some goals which they come to find is desirable.

　　– Ordway Tead

A leader is a person who has the ability to get others to do what they don't want to do, and like it.

　　– Former U.S. President Harry Truman

Charismatic Leadership

Charisma is a personal quality which results from unusual persuasive ability, power to arouse deep emotions in others, and espousal of one or more causes.

　　– Harold W. Boles & James A. Davenport

Charisma is unusual, radically different from the routine and the everyday; it is spontaneous in contrast to stable, established social forms; and it is a source of new forms and new movements, and hence creative in a fundamental sociological sense.

　　– Thomas F. O'Dea

Charisma is the unusual quality of personal magnetism possessed by the gifted leader as it is used to arouse deep emotional and volitional responses in the lives of his followers toward the end of accomplishing the predetermined objectives of his movement.

　　– J. Douglas J. Porter

Charisma in the narrower and original sense is the state or quality of being produced by receipt of the gifts of grace.

　　– Edward Shils

The term charisma does not refer to the pentecostal manifesta-
tions of tongues, miracles or other phenomena surrounding the
alleged "second blessing." The term is used by sociologists to
designate personal magnetism used by leaders to accomplish a
predetermined goal in their organization or movement.

    − Elmer L. Towns

(Charisma is) a certain quality of an individual personality by
virtue of an individual personality by virtue of which he is set
apart form ordinary men and treated as endowed with super-
natural, superhuman or at least specifically exceptional powers
or qualities. These are such as are not accessible to the ordinary
person but are regarded as of divine origin or as exemplary, and
on the basis of them the individual concerned is treated as a
leader.

    − Max Weber

Spiritual Gift of Administration

The Spirit-given capacity and desire to serve God by organizing,
administering, promoting, and leading the various affairs of the
church. The person who leads the church and its ministries.

    − Larry Gilbert

The motivation to coordinate the activities of others for the
achievement of common goals.

    − Bill Gothard

The person with this gift has the ability to perceive needs, or-
ganize and administer programs, then evaluate the results in
light of biblical objectives.

    − Elmer Towns

Miscellaneous Descriptions

There are only three kinds of people in the world – those that are immovable, those that are movable, and those that move them!

    – Li Hung Chang

It occurs to me that perhaps the best test of whether one is a qualified leader, is to find out whether anyone is following him.

    – D. E. Hoste

He who thinketh he leadeth and no one is following, is just taking a walk.

    – Old Chinese Proverb

*The word leader is translated from **proithme**, "to go before." It comes from **pro** "before" and **ithme** "to stand." It carries the idea of guide, model, and communicator – all functions of those who are before people.*

    – Elmer Towns

DICTIONARY
of Terms in This Text

Accountability, The Law of: People will follow a leader who gives them responsibility to help reach the objective. Therefore, the leader must know how followers can contribute to help reach the goal and keep up with their progress, "People don't do what you expect, but what you inspect."

Bandwagon, The Law of the: People want to be on the winning team or with the group that is going places. Therefore, leaders must have a goal the people want, reward the people who strive for the goal, be a credible example of the goal, communicate the dream plan and tactics of reaching it to the followers, and inspect where the people are and what they are doing to reach the goal. When this happens, leaders create a bandwagon attitude among their followers that motives them to greater loyalty.

Blessability, The Law of: This law states that God does not necessarily bless doctrine, programs, methods or avoidance of sin. He blesses those who are close to His heart in love, faith, and hope.

Causation, The Law of: This law states that nothing in the work of God just happens. It is all caused.

Communication, The Law of: People will follow a leader who effectively communicates his or her plan to reach the objective. Therefore, a leader must effectively communicate his/her plans and give clear directions to his/her followers.

Credibility, The Law of: When people have confidence in a leader, they will follow him and his plans; therefore, a leader must have a credibility plan to reach the objective. First of all, a leader must believe in his followers in order for them to believe in him.

Decision-Making, The Law of: People will follow a leader who gives answers to the decisions involving their objective. Therefore, a good leader must make good decisions that move followers toward the objective. Leaders must have their facts together in order to make good decisions because leaders make good decisions on good information, bad decisions on bad information, and lucky decisions on no information.

Division of Labor, The Law of the: This law states that you cannot do the work God has reserved as His own task and God will not do the work for you that He has given as your task. God has His role and we have our role.

Dreams, The Law of: People will follow a leader who directs them toward a desirable objective; therefore, the leader must direct his or her followers to the desired objective. When people buy into the leader's dreams, they buy into their leadership.

Follow-the leader mentality: Some leaders are reluctant to make a decision until other leaders have made a decision first. Then they follow the other leaders' decision instead of basing their own decision on their own knowledge and common sense.

Illustration, The Law of: People usually identify with the people in stories they hear and imagine they can experience the same results. Jesus used this law when He told parables.

Laws, The Law of: This law states that God does not run His work by chance, but by His laws. We prosper as we follow His laws and encounter difficulty when we violate these laws.

Management by Objectives (MBO):   Leading a company or ministry by focusing on objectives and basing decisions upon the objectives.

Motivation, The Law of: People will follow a leader who gives them compelling reasons to reach the objective. Therefore, the leader must communicate with and motivate followers to accomplish the objective. People follow when they have a reason to do so.

Pastor-Dictator: A church leader who owns the work, owns the facilities, and thinks he owns the people.

Pastor-Leader: A church leader who has learned to share his leadership with his people through shared decision-making, shared problem-solving, and shared goal-setting.

Peer Pressure, The Law of: People often follow the influence of others within their peer group or support group. Therefore, effective leaders learn how to use peer pressure to motivate group members who might otherwise impede the group's progress.

Praeto Principle (80/20), The: Twenty percent of your people will be leaders and eighty percent of them are followers. The dream will flow down from the twenty percent to the others. Therefore, a leader should spend eighty percent of his or her time with the twenty percent of his or her followers who demonstrate the greatest potential for leadership. A pastor is a leader of leaders who in turn lead the people.

Problem-Solving, The Law of: People will follow a leader who gives solutions to problems that hinder them from reaching their objective. Therefore, the leader must solve problems and remove barriers that frustrate followers.

Prophetic Seer: Prophetic seers were Old Testament prophets who led the nations and spoke for God. They saw first, saw furthest into the future, and saw most. They were effective leaders because they had a vision and set out to follow it. The Bible tells us, "Where there is no vision, the people perish" (Prov. 29:18).

Rewards, The Law of: People will follow a leader who rewards them from their self-chosen goals; therefore, the leader must reward those who follow him. In other words, the things that get rewarded, get done.

Seven Touches, The Law of: Research suggests that people are more likely to return for a second and third visit to a church if they are contacted by the church seven times during the weeks following their first visit. This can be done through letters, phone calls, and in-home visits.

SMART goals: SMART is an acrostic to help help remember the steps to preparing goals. Make sure goals are: **S**pecific, **M**easurable, **A**ttainable, **R**ealistic, **T**ime-Related.

Soft Soap, The Law of: This law recognizes that some people are more responsive when they are encouraged rather than rebuked. Use praise, recognition, and a show of love or support to motivate people. However, if all a leader ever does is praise the followers, those followers will not be equipped to live in the real world, so use "soft soap" in moderation.

Statistics, The Law of: Most people will respond to an idea when they realize how often it works. When facts are applied and illustrated, they can move people to actions.

Team: A team is a group of people who work together, walk together, and talk together about a common goal. There must be a common goal and an open line of communication.

Testimony, The Law of: Most people respond to the confident leader who shares how he or she has successfully done what he or she asks others to do. Testimonies motivate others to go and do likewise.

Three Hearings, The Law of: Research suggests that the average person will attend a church about three times before committing to the church.

Whip, The Law of the: Some people are only motivated to a certain course of action when pressured by fear or guilt. They do something to escape the consequences or punishment of their current action. This law should be used sparingly to motivate people to a correct response.

A TEAM effort to help train leaders in your church...

TEAM Leadership is designed to complement and enhance your present leadership skills and help you train leaders and potential leaders in your church to be great leaders through applying biblical principles of leadership. Your church leaders must join together in a team effort to lead and teach others to "do the work of the ministry" for God's glory and your church's gain.

The packet was created to help you teach the course yearly or give each future leader who has not attended the course a textbook and lesson handouts and let them borrow the cassettes to build their leadership skills.

The packet includes this textbook; a step-by-step planning agenda with fold-out calendar; teaching helps with instructions, answers and lesson handouts; a *Spiritual*

Gifts Inventory; a *L-E-A-D Personality Inventory*; a promotion section with suggested announcements, sample letters, and posters; and three audiocassettes of the eight lessons being taught by Dr. Elmer Towns.

An optional videocassette is also available.

To Order: Sign, Clip, and Mail Order Form Below or call 1-800-553-GROW

- ◻ **YES,** send me the TEAM Leadership resource packet (Order No. 421) at $69.95 each, plus shipping and handling ($4.50 [$5.50 Canada]).
- ◻ **YES,** send me the optional TEAM Leadership videocassette (sound track on audiotape and videotape are the same) (Order No. 421V) at $29.95 each, plus shipping and handling ($4.50 [$5.50 Canada]).

Order Amount..........$ _____
S & H......................$ _____
VA residents add
4 1/2% sales tax ....$ _____
Total ....$ _____

◻ Payment enclosed.
◻ Please bill church.

Signature _____
Title _____

Name _____
Your position in church_____
Church _____ Attendance _____
Address_____
City _____ Phone _____
State _____ Zip _____

Church Growth Institute
Providing Practical Tools for Growth
P.O. Box 4404, Lynchburg, VA 24502